When I See Performance... I Hear Music!
　　　　　　　　　　Nagy Salib

To my sons, David and Daniel
May your lives always play in harmony, guided by faith, courage, and kindness.

The Symphony of Success

Orchestrating Your Performance and Growth

By Nagy A. Salib, MBA, MSc

A journey towards personal & professional development

Everyday Life

NAGY A. SALIB - BCom, MSc, MBA
When I see Performance, I hear Music

The Symphony of Success
Orchestrating Your Performance and Growth

Copyright © 2025 by Nagy A. Salib

All rights reserved. No part of this book may be reproduced, distributed, or transmitted in any form or by any means, including photocopying, recording, or other electronic or mechanical methods, without the prior written permission of the publisher, except in the case of brief quotations embodied in critical reviews and certain other non-commercial uses permitted by copyright law.

For permission requests, contact the publisher at:
Scholatic – Education Consulting Services
nagy@scholatic.org

ISBN (Paperback): 978-1-0697407-1-7
ISBN (eBook): 978-1-0697407-2-4

First Edition, 2025

Preface

In a world filled with distractions and noise, finding your personal rhythm can feel like a challenge. But much like music, life offers a melody waiting to be discovered.

Throughout my career, I've met many people standing at life's crossroads, unsure of which path to take, doubting their abilities, and unaware of the potential within them. Yet, with the right guidance, I've seen them rise higher than they ever imagined, discovering strengths they never believed they had. Their transformation is proof that, when nurtured, every life carries a symphony waiting to be played.

Inspired by the power of music and the lessons of leadership, The Symphony of Success invites you to tune your life, collaborate with others, and lead with intention.

About the Author
Nagy A. Salib, B.Com., MSc, MBA

A seasoned education and business professional with over 30 years of experience in higher education management, professional development, and management consulting. With a Bachelor of Commerce, a Master of Science in Management, and a Master of Business Administration in International Business, Nagy brings a unique combination of academic expertise and real-world insights to his work.

As a multilingual and multicultural professional, Nagy has lived and worked across the Middle East, North America, and Canada, while travelling extensively to numerous countries across the Americas, Europe, Africa, Asia, and the Arabian Gulf. These experiences have shaped his global perspective and deepened his understanding of diverse cultural and professional landscapes.

Driven by a mission to "help people find their way," Nagy has dedicated his career to teaching, training, mentoring, and empowering people at various stages of their lives, education, and careers.

Starting his journey as an international student in the United States, Nagy's personal and professional experiences have made him a dedicated advocate for guiding others through the challenges and opportunities of growth. His insights into overcoming transitions and building transferable skills have become the foundation of his philosophy and success.

Why "The Symphony of Success"?

Success, like music, is never made from a single note. It's a composition, an intricate blend of sound, silence, rhythm, timing, and harmony. *The Symphony of Success* is a metaphor for how we must learn to orchestrate our lives intentionally, thoughtfully, and with purpose.

Each of us carries within us a set of instruments: Our talents, education, experiences, values, our passions, and our aspirations. On their own, each element might make noise. But when aligned, tuned to the same purpose and guided by a clear vision, they make music. Not just any music, but a personal, powerful, and moving symphony that reflects who we are and what we're capable of achieving.

In an orchestra, not every instrument plays at once, and not every part is loud. The art lies in coordination, timing, and knowing when to lead and when to listen. The same is true for life. We don't need to be perfect at everything, but we do need to know how to align our strengths and address our gaps, when to push forward and when to pause, when to collaborate and when to take the lead.

Ultimately, we are each our own maestro. No one else can conduct the orchestra of your life. It's up to you to bring out the best in every part of yourself, to fine-tune your direction, and to create harmony in the way you learn, grow, contribute, and lead.

This book is your guide to doing just that; To recognize your instruments, tune them, and lead them.

What inspired me to write this book

It all started with a piano that wasn't even mine.

I was maybe five years old when my dad bought my sister a piano and hired a teacher. I wasn't part of the lesson plan, but I sat there quietly every week, absorbing the sounds. Even back then, something clicked: music just made sense. Not logically, but emotionally. It moved, it flowed, and I instinctively followed.

I didn't know how to read music. Honestly, I didn't care at this point. I just played by ear, chasing the melodies I'd heard, trying to recreate the feelings they gave me. When my sister's lesson ended, I'd jump on the piano, pressing keys until it sounded right. And somehow, it often did.

Later, I fell in love with the guitar and decided to study formally at the conservatory. I decided to learn how to read music, and it opened up an entirely new dimension. I discovered structure, depth, and expression beyond instinct. But even with all that knowledge, one thing still mattered most: feeling the music.

I practiced relentlessly, not because I had to, but because I couldn't not. I imagined people dancing to the songs I played. Every note had to mean something. I wasn't just playing; I was telling stories without words.

When it came to playing with others, it was a whole different challenge; It felt limiting!

Suddenly, I wasn't the center of the show. I had to match tempo, tone, and timing. I had to listen. I had to let go of control. And worst of all (at the time), I had to follow a conductor who seemed to control everything - from when to start, to how loud or soft I should play.

It was frustrating. But then... I saw it.

When we all played together, something bigger emerged. The same music I once played solo now had texture, weight, and richness. I realized the conductor wasn't controlling us; he was guiding us. Like a lighthouse, he kept us aligned, helping each of us shine in a coordinated, powerful performance.

Years later, I found myself in corporate settings - training, teaching, managing teams. And guess what? I saw the same dynamics. Individual talent is important, but real success comes when we play in harmony. Leading a team, a project, a life, it's all a form of music. One that requires you to master your own rhythm while staying in tune with others.

This book helps you tune your life like an instrument. To move from independence to interdependence. To find your rhythm, join the ensemble, and - when you're ready - lead like a maestro.

About the Book

In Symphony, Nagy Salib uses music as a powerful metaphor to explore the universal journey of personal and professional development. The book takes readers through three essential stages of growth:

1. **Independence:** Achieving individual effectiveness through personal mastery.
2. **Interdependence:** Thriving as part of a team by mastering collaboration and teamwork.
3. **Leadership:** Transitioning to lead oneself and others with purpose and harmony.

Drawing on his extensive experience, Nagy simplifies complex concepts and provides actionable insights for each stage of growth. The book highlights the challenges, opportunities, and mindset shifts needed to navigate these transitions, ensuring readers can adapt and grow in meaningful ways.

Through relatable anecdotes, practical tips, and thought-provoking ideas, "The Symphony" guides readers in orchestrating their unique instruments of skills, knowledge, and resources. By achieving a dynamic balance, readers are empowered to perform at the highest level, achieving harmony in life, learning, career, relationships, and personal fulfilment.

Whether you're seeking clarity in personal growth, teamwork dynamics, or leadership effectiveness, "The Symphony" offers a roadmap to help you unlock your potential and create a life of meaning and success.

When I see Performance, I hear music!

A Journey of Growth, Collaboration, and Leadership

Life is like a symphony, a masterpiece unfolding in movements, where every note, rhythm, and harmony plays a role in shaping the final performance. In this transformative book, readers embark on a journey of self-discovery, teamwork, and leadership, guided by the metaphor of a symphony. The book invites you to create your own unique symphony of success, blending personal growth, collaboration, and leadership into a legacy of impact.

Tuning Your Instrument – The Art of Self-Discovery

The symphony begins with self-discovery, much like a musician mastering their instrument. Before you can contribute to a larger ensemble, you must first understand your unique strengths, values, and aspirations.

Through self-awareness, reflection, and deliberate practice, you align your actions with your core principles, turning raw potential into achievement. Like tuning an instrument, personal mastery demands resilience, consistency, and an openness to learning. Every challenge becomes a chance to fine-tune your skills, transforming setbacks into steppingstones.

Playing your solo is where you embrace your individuality and craft a melody that's uniquely yours.

Harmonizing with Others – The Power of Collaboration

True progress begins when individual mastery evolves into teamwork. Collaboration is the heartbeat of any symphony, where musicians align their parts to create a unified, harmonious sound. In life, this means learning to listen with intention, communicate with clarity, and adapt with empathy.

Teamwork thrives on interdependence, a shared commitment to collective success. By blending your strengths with those of others, you contribute to something greater than yourself. Here is where your melody becomes part of a larger composition, enriched by the contributions of those around you.

Conducting the Orchestra – The Rise of Leadership

Leadership is the final movement of this journey, the moment where all elements come together to create something extraordinary. A conductor doesn't play an instrument but shapes the entire orchestra's performance with vision, trust, and adaptability. Similarly, great leaders inspire and empower others, fostering environments where creativity and collaboration can thrive.

Leadership isn't about control; it's about guiding others to achieve shared goals while allowing them the autonomy to shine. Your role as a leader is to ensure that every voice is heard and every individual is empowered to play their best.

Embracing Imperfection and Change

Like any symphony, life has unexpected shifts, moments of discord that challenge your rhythm. But within these moments lies the opportunity for growth and resilience. Embracing imperfection and vulnerability adds depth and authenticity to your journey.

The true beauty of a symphony isn't in its flawless execution but in its ability to connect people, tell stories, and evoke emotion.

Your life's symphony is no different.

Each of us is both composer and performer of our life's masterpiece. This book invites you to take ownership of that role, crafting a melody that reflects your authentic self while contributing to the greater harmony of your community and the world.

By applying the lessons and tools shared, you'll compose a life of purpose, passion, and impact. Your symphony, performed with heart and intention, will resonate far beyond your lifetime, a testament to the transformative power of growth, collaboration, and leadership.

So, pick up your baton, tune your instrument, and step onto the stage. The world is ready to hear your symphony.

Table of Contents

About the Author 5

Preface 4

About the Book... 9

Introduction 14

Chapter 1 17

Self-Discovery: Master Your Independence 17

Chapter 2 84

From Independent to Interdependent 84

Achieving Performance Mastery as Part of a Group 84

Chapter 3 103

Lead Like a Maestro... 103

Chapter 4 125

How Your Thoughts Can Impact Your Growth 125

Chapter 5 158

The Fine Line 158

Final Notes 167

Introduction

Have you ever watched a master musician at work—not just hearing the notes, but feeling every movement, every breath, every moment of connection between their body and the instrument? That kind of mastery doesn't come from talent alone. It comes from deep understanding, relentless practice, and passion that transcends perfection.

Now, imagine picking up a new instrument for the first time. Before you can create beautiful music, you must learn how it works—its range, its strengths, its limitations. With time, you move from clumsy attempts to smooth melodies, and eventually to powerful performances. Yet even then, what moves people isn't just your technical skill; it's your passion, your connection to the music, and your ability to communicate something meaningful.

Now, imagine that the instrument is you. Your life is your song. Your skills, values, and dreams are the notes. To bring out your best performance, you must start with self-discovery. Just like a musician becomes intimately familiar with their instrument, you must take the time to understand your unique rhythm, your strengths and weaknesses, your fears and aspirations, your calling.

This book is your guide to that journey. *The Symphony of Success* is about more than setting goals or achieving results. It's about aligning who you are with what you do and learning to orchestrate your growth with purpose and clarity.

To begin that journey, you need to start asking yourself the right questions:

- What are your natural talents?
- What inspires and excites you?
- What challenges you?
- What kind of impact do you want your life to have?

Without self-awareness, it's easy to feel out of tune, disconnected, frustrated, or lost in the noise of expectations and comparison. But when you understand your instrument, your rhythm, your voice, you begin to create a melody that resonates, not just with others, but deeply within yourself.

Playing in Harmony

Even the most brilliant soloist can't match the depth and beauty of a full symphony. True growth happens not only in personal mastery but in learning how to harmonize with others.

Collaboration is like joining a band or orchestra. Every member plays a role. Each contribution, no matter how quiet or bold, shapes the overall performance. But playing in harmony doesn't come naturally; it takes practice and humility.

Working in harmony requires:

- **Listening with intention**: Seeking to truly understand others' perspectives and roles.
- **Communicating clearly**: Ensuring your voice is heard without overpowering others.
- **Adapting your part**: Adjusting to the collective rhythm while staying true to your tone.

Collaboration invites us to embrace the beauty of interdependence. It's not about losing your voice; it's about amplifying it in unity.

The Art of Leadership

Leadership is the ultimate movement in this symphony of life. Picture a Maestro standing at the front of an orchestra—not playing an instrument but bringing every musician into harmony. The conductor sees the bigger picture, feels the rhythm of the whole, and guides others toward a shared vision.

Leadership is about more than expertise; it's about vision, empathy, and influence. Great leaders don't just guide others; they create space for others to thrive, to contribute, and to grow. Leadership means aligning personal mastery and collective effort toward something greater than the sum of its parts.

Your life's symphony is yours to orchestrate. Conduct it with intention, purpose, and passion.

Chapter 1

Self-Discovery: Master Your Independence

The Journey to Success Begins with Self-Discovery

"Who are you?"

It sounds like a simple question, right? But when a wise man once asked me this, back when I was an international student in the United States, I found myself fumbling for an answer. I told him my name, but he shook his head.

"I didn't ask your name," he said. "I asked who you are."

At the time, I didn't understand. I had approached him to teach me martial arts, expecting straightforward lessons on technique and discipline. Instead, he asked me questions that left me confused.

He continued, "Before I teach you, I want to know the man I'm going to teach. Take time to think about your values, your thoughts, your skills, hobbies, and limitations. Reflect on what you're doing and why. Think about what makes you happy, sad, or angry - and why?"

I was still puzzled. "Why are you asking me all of this? I just want to learn martial arts!"

The wise man smiled and replied, "You want me to teach you something powerful and potentially dangerous. I need to know how you'll use it. To master these skills, you must first master yourself—your thoughts, emotions, desires, and weaknesses. Knowing who you are is the foundation of all learning. Take your time, because self-discovery is the beginning of your journey."

A Moment That Changed Everything

I was 26 years old when this conversation happened, and it completely shifted my perspective on life. It opened a door to a deeper understanding of myself; my values, my purpose, and my vision.

I realized that before I could excel in any field or make meaningful choices, I needed to know who I truly was.

This process of self-awareness didn't stop at reflection—it transformed how I thought, what I prioritized, and the goals I pursued. With a clearer sense of identity, I began to align my decisions with what mattered most and where I wanted to go.

The Next Step

Self-discovery is only the beginning. Once you understand your strengths, weaknesses, and passions, the next step is to develop your abilities.

This means honing your skills, nurturing your talents, and working on areas that need improvement. Just like a musician spends hours perfecting their craft, we must invest time and effort into growing into who we are meant to be.

For some, this might involve studying, practicing, or seeking mentorship. For others, it may mean stepping outside of comfort zones and facing challenges head-on. Growth doesn't happen by accident; it requires intention, courage, and the resolve to push through discomfort.

The journey of self-development isn't easy. There will be setbacks and frustrations. But these moments shape resilience, patience, and adaptability. Just like a musician improves with daily practice, we grow stronger through consistent effort.

When you commit to refining your abilities, you equip yourself not only to pursue your goals but to meet life's challenges with confidence.

Knowing your strengths and values is essential to making wise, informed decisions. It allows you to choose paths - whether in education, career, or personal life - that align with who you are and what truly matters.

When you truly understand yourself, you can navigate life with clarity and purpose. You'll make decisions that not only lead to success but also bring fulfilment.

Self-discovery is the secret ingredient to unlocking both personal and professional growth. Why? Because it's the compass that guides your choices, whether those choices involve your education, career, or life goals. Knowing who you truly are isn't just some abstract concept; it's the foundation for living a life filled with purpose and direction. When you tap into your own self-awareness, you're empowered to make smarter and more intentional decisions about your future.

> *"True self-discovery begins with the courage to be honest about who you are today, so you can grow into who you're meant to become tomorrow. Honesty in self-discovery is not about judgment, but about clarity."*

By diving deep into your interests, you can identify the subjects, hobbies, and career paths that truly light you up. This means that your journey becomes more than just a series of tasks; it transforms into an exciting exploration of what you love. Knowing what you're good at allows you to lean into your strengths, but it's also crucial to be aware of your limitations. When you understand where you can grow, you create a roadmap for improvement that feels not only achievable but also meaningful. This self-awareness empowers you to take on challenges with confidence, knowing that each step is part of a bigger picture.

Self-discovery isn't a one-time event; it's a continuous journey. As you grow, learn, and change, your sense of self will evolve. With a strong understanding of your core values and strengths, you can pivot, explore new opportunities, and adjust your path when needed.

It's this adaptability that allows you to thrive, no matter what life throws your way.

So, ask yourself: "Who am I?"
The answer might just change everything.

Exploring Yourself: Using SWOT for Self-Discovery

Self-discovery is a journey, an ongoing process of understanding your identity, values, and vision. While personal reflection is important, it can sometimes be difficult to organize your thoughts or gain clarity on where you stand.

That's where self-assessment tools come in. They offer structure, helping you examine your strengths, weaknesses, values, and preferences with greater focus. These insights can reveal patterns, open new perspectives, and guide your goal-setting in meaningful ways.

By using tools like SWOT analysis, you can better understand yourself and take purposeful steps toward personal growth.

SWOT analysis is a simple yet powerful tool for self-discovery. You might recognize it from the business world, but its strength lies in how effectively it can be adapted for personal growth.

It helps you step back, examine your internal and external world, and make clearer, more intentional decisions about your development.

What is SWOT?

S – Strengths: What are you naturally good at? What qualities or skills do others often recognize in you?

W – Weaknesses: Where do you struggle? What habits or patterns limit your growth or confidence?

O – Opportunities: What resources, relationships, or circumstances can you take advantage of to move forward?

T – Threats: What external challenges or internal fears could hold you back from progress?

By breaking your experiences into these four categories, you gain a clearer view of where you stand, where you can grow, and what might need attention. SWOT is more than a list; it's a personal mirror that helps you better understand your current path and navigate it with purpose.

Let's explore how you can use the **SWOT** tool on your self-discovery journey.

Step 1: Find Your Strengths

Understanding your strengths is the first step in recognizing your potential. These are the areas where you naturally excel or feel proud of what you've accomplished.

Ask yourself:
- **What am I really good at?** (e.g., sports, writing, problem-solving, helping others)

- **What do my friends, family, or mentors say I excel in?**
- **What's an achievement I'm genuinely proud of?**

Examples:
- *"I'm great at public speaking and negotiating."*
- *"I'm creative and love drawing."*

Identifying your strengths allows you to build on what already makes you shine. These strengths can guide your goals, boost your confidence, and shape how you contribute to the world.

Step 2: Recognize Your Weaknesses

We all have areas where we struggle, and acknowledging them is not a flaw, but a powerful step toward growth. When you recognize your weaknesses, you open the door to self-improvement and personal evolution.

Ask yourself:
- **What do I often struggle with?** (e.g., staying organized, managing time, speaking up)
- **What tasks or situations do I avoid because they feel intimidating or overwhelming?**
- **What feedback do I tend to receive repeatedly from others?**

Examples:
- *"I get nervous when speaking in front of others."*
- *"I sometimes procrastinate and miss deadlines."*

Acknowledging your weaknesses doesn't mean dwelling on them—it's about identifying where you can grow so you can become your best self.

Step 3: Spot Opportunities

Opportunities are all around you, often hiding in plain sight. These are the people, places, or experiences that can support your growth and help you move toward your goals.

Ask yourself:
- **Are there clubs, classes, or events I can join to learn something new?**
- **Are there mentors, teachers, or peers who can offer support or guidance?**
- **Is there something I've always wanted to try but haven't yet explored?**

Examples:
- *"I could join the debate team to improve my speaking skills."*
- *"I can take an online art class to learn new techniques."*

Opportunities are not just options, they're pathways. When you recognize and act on them, you begin to build momentum and move more confidently toward the goals you've set for yourself.

Step 4: Be Aware of Threats

Threats are the external pressures, obstacles, or circumstances that could slow you down or prevent you from reaching your goals.

While they might feel intimidating, identifying them early gives you the power to plan ahead and build resilience.

Ask yourself:
- **What stresses me out or consistently holds me back?** (e.g., distractions, fear of failure)
- **Are there external pressures—like competition, comparison, or expectations—that make me feel uneasy?**
- **Is anything actively preventing me from pursuing my goals or staying consistent?**

Examples:
- *"I don't have enough time to balance school and soccer practice."*
- *"I compare myself to others, and it makes me feel discouraged."*

Recognizing your threats doesn't mean you have to accept them as limits. It means you're becoming more aware and more equipped to develop strategies that reduce their impact and keep you moving forward.

Using a SWOT analysis helps you see yourself more clearly. It's like holding up a mirror - not just to your strengths - but also to the areas where you can grow. With this clarity, you're better equipped to:
- Set realistic and meaningful goals.
- Build on your strengths to create new opportunities.

- Develop a focused plan to address your weaknesses.
- Anticipate obstacles and prepare strategies to navigate them.

Self-discovery is a lifelong journey, but tools like SWOT make that path more visible. They help you understand where you are today - and more importantly - where you're capable of going.

Your SWOT analysis isn't just a snapshot; it's a roadmap for growth and evolution.

Create a Plan Forward

Now that you've identified your strengths, weaknesses, opportunities, and threats, it's time to turn those insights into action.

Ask yourself:

- **How can I leverage my strengths to take advantage of opportunities?**
- **What specific steps can I take to improve in the areas where I struggle?**
- **How can I prepare for, reduce, or overcome the threats that stand in my way?**

By answering these questions, you begin to transform awareness into intention, and intention into meaningful progress.

Your SWOT analysis isn't something you do just once. Think of it as a living document - a reflection of who you are and who you're becoming. Revisit it regularly, perhaps every few months, to assess your progress and update your goals.

You may find that a weakness has become a new strength, or that fresh opportunities have appeared that weren't visible before.

These regular check-ins help you stay aligned with your evolving path. Growth is not a straight line; it's a series of adjustments, lessons, and breakthroughs.

Use your SWOT analysis as a guide, not a rigid framework. Be flexible. Celebrate your progress. Learn from your setbacks. And most importantly, stay curious about your potential.

Every intentional step - no matter how small - moves you forward. Take what you've learned, reflect deeply, and begin shaping the future you truly want to create.

Sample SWOT Chart

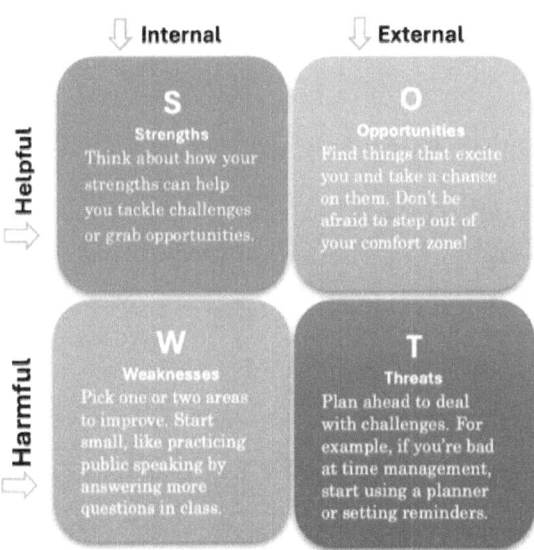

The Power of Self-Discovery

Self-discovery is the cornerstone of both personal and professional growth, because knowing who you are directly shapes the choices you make. From the education you pursue to the career paths you follow, your sense of self guides how you show up in the world.

This isn't just an abstract idea. It's the foundation of a purposeful life. When you understand what excites you and where your natural talents lie, you're able to make choices that align with your goals, values, and vision for the future. Tools like SWOT analysis help bring that self-awareness into sharper focus.

- **Explore What Inspires You:** When you identify your genuine interests, your educational and career decisions become more engaging and more sustainable. You're no longer chasing someone else's version of success. You're tuning into what fuels your curiosity and drive.

- **Focus on Strengths and Growth Areas:** Recognizing your strengths helps you move with confidence, while acknowledging your limitations creates space for learning and progress. This self-knowledge makes your goals feel grounded, achievable, and personally meaningful.

- **Stay Flexible as You Grow:** Self-discovery isn't a one-time event; it evolves as you do. When you stay connected to your core values and emerging talents, you're better equipped to pivot when needed, seize new opportunities, and reshape your journey with purpose.

Ultimately, self-discovery turns growth into something greater than a checklist. It becomes a lifelong process of composing a life filled with intention, joy, and momentum.

Breaking Free from Self-Limiting Beliefs

Self-discovery is powerful—but it's not always easy. Often, the path forward is blocked not by a lack of ability, but by quiet internal forces: the stories we tell ourselves about who we are and what we're capable of.

These self-limiting beliefs, like *"I'm not good enough,"* or *"I'll never succeed,"* often come from past failures, painful experiences, or even the subtle weight of cultural and societal expectations. Over time, these beliefs can feel like truths, even when they're not.

Here's how they can hold you back:

- **They weaken your confidence:** These thoughts make you second-guess your abilities and shy away from challenges that could lead to growth.
- **They keep you stuck:** Fear of failure or rejection may keep you in your comfort zone, preventing meaningful progress.

- **They isolate you:** Beliefs like *"I don't belong,"* or *"People won't accept me,"* can cause you to pull away from others, missing out on connection and support.

Recognizing these patterns is the first step toward freeing yourself from them. Because once you understand that a belief is just a thought - not a fact - you gain the power to change it.

The Good News

The beliefs that hold you back don't have to define you. With awareness and intention, you can begin to replace them with thoughts that empower rather than limit you. Here's how to start:

1. **Identify and Challenge Your Beliefs**

    Notice the negative thoughts you repeat to yourself. Ask: *Is this really true? Where did it come from? Would I say this to someone I care about?* Often, these beliefs are rooted in fear, not fact.

2. **Revisit Your SWOT Analysis**

    Look at the strengths you've identified and view your weaknesses as areas for development, not fixed flaws. This helps shift your mindset from judgment to growth.

3. **Build Confidence Through Small Wins**

    Celebrate progress in small steps. Each success - no matter how minor - reinforces your ability to change. And when fear strikes, ask yourself: *What's the worst that could really happen?* You'll often find it's far less overwhelming than it seems.

4. **Embrace a Growth Mindset**

   Instead of seeing challenges as proof of inadequacy, treat them as learning opportunities. Failure doesn't define you, effort does.

5. **Seek Encouraging Support**

   Surround yourself with people who believe in your potential. Whether it's a mentor, friend, or coach, the right voices can help you challenge doubt and stay accountable to your growth.

Breaking free from limiting beliefs takes time, reflection, and courage, but the reward is worth it: greater confidence, deeper resilience, and a stronger, more authentic sense of self.

Mastery: Becoming Your Best Self

Once you've embraced self-discovery and begun to overcome your self-limiting beliefs, the next step is mastery. But mastery isn't simply about perfecting a skill; it's about becoming fully aligned with your values, your passions, and your purpose.

Think of a musician. True mastery isn't about hitting every note perfectly; it's about pouring emotion into the music, crafting something that resonates, not just performs. The same is true for life. Mastery is about living with depth, intention, and authenticity. It's about showing up as your best self and offering your unique gifts to the world.

How to Achieve Mastery

- **Stay Dedicated:** Mastery takes time, practice, and perseverance. Consistency beats intensity over the long haul.
- **Celebrate Progress:** Every step counts. Acknowledge your growth, however small, and let it fuel your momentum.
- **Keep Learning:** Mastery isn't a final destination; it's a lifelong journey. Stay curious. Stay open. Stay evolving.

When your actions align with your values and passions, life begins to feel like a symphony - rich, harmonious, and deeply fulfilling. You're no longer just performing tasks; you're living on purpose.

The Journey of a Lifetime

Self-discovery, personal development, and mastery aren't events you check off a list; they're lifelong journeys. Like a musician who must regularly tune their instrument, we too must continue to reflect, refine, and realign ourselves with who we are and where we're going.

Embrace the journey. Explore your identity. Challenge the beliefs that no longer serve you. And above all, commit to creating a life that reflects the fullest version of who you're becoming. When you do, the possibilities ahead are limitless.

Managing Change

One of the only constants in life is change. Sometimes it creeps in gradually, and other times it arrives without warning. Whether it's a planned transition or an unexpected shift, learning to navigate change is a skill that empowers growth and resilience.

Change invites us to stretch, to leave behind the familiar, and to step into the unknown. While it often brings fresh possibilities, it can also challenge our sense of identity, stability, or confidence. How we respond - whether with resistance or with curiosity - can make all the difference between feeling stuck and moving forward with strength.

The Many Faces of Change

Change wears many faces. Sometimes it unfolds slowly; like the quiet evolution of technology or shifting cultural norms. Other times, it arrives abruptly: a career transition, a personal loss, a new opportunity, or even a global event that shakes the ground beneath us.

Change can be driven by external forces: economic shifts, scientific discoveries, or workplace dynamics. But it can also come from within, sparked by a hunger for growth, a shift in values, or a vision of a better life. Regardless of its origin, change often disrupts the familiar and invites us to evolve in ways we didn't expect.

The Challenges of Change

But change rarely feels simple. Even when it leads to something positive, it can provoke discomfort. Stepping into unfamiliar territory can trigger resistance, anxiety, or even fear. This is natural - our comfort zones exist for a reason. They give us a sense of control and safety.

Yet it's in those moments of disruption that we're offered something powerful: the chance to grow. Discomfort becomes a teacher, showing us how to adapt, how to become more resilient, and how to stretch into our potential. When we accept change as part of life's rhythm, we begin to meet it with curiosity instead of fear.

While change can feel intimidating, it's also one of the most powerful catalysts for growth. It pushes us to evolve, adapt, and expand beyond the limits of our comfort zones. Change invites us to:

- **Learn new skills:** Adapting often means gaining fresh knowledge or developing new abilities that enrich our toolkit.
- **Push boundaries:** Change challenges us to think differently, stretch beyond the familiar, and reimagine what's possible.
- **Build resilience:** Every time we navigate change successfully, we gain confidence in our ability to handle life's uncertainties.

Though it may disrupt your routines, change also opens doors to new opportunities, relationships, and experiences that can shape your path in powerful and meaningful ways.

Change is inevitable. It sparks progress, drives innovation, and creates space for transformation. But let's be honest, change isn't always smooth, and it's not always positive. From fear of the unknown to conflicting goals, the emotional and practical hurdles of change can feel overwhelming. Even more importantly, not all change is aligned with growth. Some changes can distract, derail, or deplete us if we don't approach them with clarity and purpose.

So, how do we begin to distinguish between change that leads to meaningful development and change that simply leads us astray?

Common Challenges of Change

As you consider making meaningful changes in your life, it's important to recognize what might stand in your way.

Here are some of the most common challenges that arise:

- **Fear of the Unknown**: Stepping into unfamiliar territory can trigger anxiety and hesitation. It often feels safer to stick with what we know, even if it's no longer serving us.
- **Attachment to Comfort Zones**: Routines, habits, and predictability offer a sense of control and safety. Letting go of that comfort can feel like losing a part of yourself.

- **Emotional and Physical Adjustment**: Change can be mentally draining and physically disruptive, affecting everything from your energy levels to your emotional stability.
- **Conflict with Priorities**: Change doesn't happen in a vacuum; it often intersects with existing responsibilities or group goals, creating internal or external tension.

These obstacles are part of why change can feel so overwhelming, but they also reveal just how much potential lies on the other side. When we acknowledge and prepare for these challenges, we increase our capacity to grow through them.

Not Every Change Leads to Progress

It's easy to assume that all change brings growth, but that's not always true. Some changes, even when well-meaning, can create setbacks, waste energy, or cause long-term dissatisfaction. That's why it's critical to assess change with clarity and purpose before moving forward. Consider the following missteps:

- **Change Misaligned with Core Goals**: If a change doesn't align with your personal, professional, or societal vision, it can scatter your focus and resources. For example, pursuing a new job that seems exciting in the moment but doesn't support your long-term goals may ultimately lead to frustration or disconnection.

- **Poor Planning and Execution**: Even positive ideas can fail when rushed. Without a clear strategy, preparation, or communication, change can lead to confusion, burnout, or widespread resistance.
- **Short-Term Thinking**: Some changes bring fast results but set up long-term problems. Focusing only on immediate success, such as hitting quick metrics in a project, can create instability or inefficiencies over time.
- **Conflict with Personal or Shared Values**: Change that violates your principles, ethics, or cultural integrity can lead to regret and broken trust. When change undermines what matters most, progress becomes hollow.
- **Imposing Change Without Input**: When changes are made without involving those they impact, it often leads to resistance, confusion, or resentment.
- **Misdiagnosing the Problem**: Jumping into action without fully understanding the core issue often results in wasted time and effort. Before initiating change, take time to investigate root causes rather than reacting to symptoms.
- **Overloading with Multiple Changes**: Attempting too many initiatives at once, especially without a phased approach, can overwhelm teams, systems, or even your own emotional capacity. Prioritization is key to sustainable progress.

- **Disruption of Relationships**: Change that affects interpersonal dynamics, such as abrupt shifts in leadership style or expectations, can erode trust and collaboration. Open dialogue and emotional intelligence are vital when change intersects with relationships.
- **Unnecessary Complexity**: Sometimes, change adds layers of complication instead of improving outcomes. Simplifying processes or focusing on essential improvements often yields better, more lasting results.
- **Change for the Sake of Change**: Making changes impulsively or simply out of boredom can conflict with commitments to family, work, or community. Sustainable change should always serve a larger purpose or strategic vision, not just a fleeting desire.

Thoughtful change demands self-awareness, clear communication, and purposeful planning. Without these, even well-intended shifts can create more friction than growth.

How to Approach Change Thoughtfully

To avoid the common pitfalls of misguided change, it's essential to approach transformation with purpose, clarity, and foresight. Here's how to evaluate whether a change is worth pursuing:
- **Align with Goals and Values**: Before initiating any change, ask whether it supports your long-term goals and stays true to

your personal or shared values. Change that lacks alignment can quickly become a distraction.
- **Plan and Communicate**: Create a clear roadmap for implementing the change. Communicate expectations, timelines, and intentions transparently with those affected. Preparation builds trust and minimizes resistance.
- **Evaluate Long-Term Impact**: Don't be swayed by short-term benefits. Ask: Will this change still feel right a year from now? What are the potential unintended consequences?
- **Involve Others**: Meaningful change should never be imposed in isolation. Seek feedback and input from the people it will affect. Inclusive decisions lead to stronger outcomes.
- **Start Small**: If possible, pilot the change on a small scale first. This allows you to test the waters, gather feedback, and adjust as needed before rolling it out more broadly.

Change, when guided by thoughtful planning and alignment with core values, becomes a catalyst for growth, not chaos. While not every change is the right change, those approached with care and intention can shape a future that reflects your highest potential.

Before embracing change, take a moment to reflect. Strategic decisions require more than momentum - they require intention.

Ask yourself:

- **Does this change align with my goals and long-term vision?**
- **Am I prepared for the challenges it may bring?**
- **Will this change add real value to my life, or is it a distraction?**

Change is rarely just a step forward or backward - it's a rebalancing act between what is gained and what might be lost. Every decision to change comes with trade-offs, and recognizing those trade-offs is essential.

By evaluating both the potential rewards and the necessary sacrifices, you equip yourself to make decisions that reflect your core values and aspirations.

What You Stand to Gain

While change can be challenging, it also opens the door to growth, learning, and alignment with your deeper purpose. Here are some of the potential rewards that thoughtful change can bring:

- **Personal Growth**: Taking on a challenge often reveals strengths and interests you didn't know you had. For example, switching careers might feel risky at first, but can lead to discovering a deeper passion and a renewed sense of purpose.
- **Skill Development**: Change often pushes us to build new competencies. Whether you're learning a language, stepping into a leadership role, or pursuing a creative hobby, each skill adds value to both your personal and professional life.

- **Opportunities for Advancement**: Embracing change can unlock new possibilities that were previously out of reach, such as promotions, new connections, or projects that align with your aspirations.
- **Stronger Alignment with Your Values**: When your life or work better reflects your core beliefs, you're more likely to experience satisfaction, motivation, and creativity. For instance, transitioning to a role that supports causes you care about can bring a deeper sense of fulfilment.

Change isn't just something to survive; it can be a gateway to a more authentic, empowered version of yourself.

What Might You Have to Let Go?

Recognizing what you may need to release is essential for making fully informed decisions.

- **Comfort and Stability:** Letting go of what's familiar can be unsettling. For example, moving to a new city might unlock career opportunities but also require starting over socially and emotionally. Are you prepared for that kind of reset?
- **Time and Energy:** Meaningful change demands commitment. Going back to school could boost your future, but it also means investing hours of study and juggling responsibilities. Do you have the bandwidth to see it through?

- **Risk of Failure:** No change is guaranteed to succeed. Launching a business or pivoting careers comes with uncertainty, and potentially financial or emotional strain. Are you comfortable with the unknown?
- **Impact on Relationships:** Personal transformation can create tension with those around you. Prioritizing new goals or values might disrupt existing dynamics with family, friends, or colleagues. Are you ready to navigate those shifts?

Change isn't inherently good or bad - it's about whether it moves you closer to the life you want. When you weigh the potential gains against what you may have to release, you're better equipped to choose a change that truly serves your purpose.

Find Your Unique Sound

Understand Your Nature and Personality

Understanding yourself is like learning to play an instrument. Before you can create something truly beautiful, you have to know how that instrument works: its tone, range, and even its limitations. In the same way, self-awareness is the foundation of personal growth and fulfillment. Without it, we can end up chasing goals or living lives that don't reflect who we really are, leaving us feeling unfulfilled or disconnected.

But self-discovery isn't a quick breakthrough or a one-time realization, it's an unfolding process. It's about peeling back layers, questioning assumptions, and becoming curious about what drives you at your core.

It's not about chasing perfection. It's about learning how to work with your strengths, understanding your tendencies, and honoring your uniqueness. When you do that, you begin to shape a life that feels like it truly belongs to you.

Take the first step: Explore, reflect, and be patient with the process. You'll be spending a lifetime with yourself, so make that relationship intentional and true. The journey might take time, but the clarity, confidence, and authenticity you gain are worth every step.

Knowing Your Strengths and Limitations

Your strengths are your unique talents and abilities; the things you naturally excel at without even trying. Recognizing these strengths allows you to develop them further and use them in ways that bring value to your life and the lives of others.

When you understand what you're good at, you can:

- **Pursue opportunities** that align with your natural talents. If you're a strong communicator, for instance, you might feel drawn to roles like public speaking, teaching, or coaching.
- **Build confidence** by leaning into what comes naturally to you. When you engage in tasks that highlight your strengths, you tend to feel more capable and motivated.

But focusing solely on strengths isn't enough. Understanding your limitations is just as important. We all have areas where we need growth, support, or improvement - and that's okay.

Knowing your limitations isn't about focusing on the negatives - it's about being honest with yourself and using that insight to make smarter choices.

When you're aware of your limitations, you can:

- **Avoid unnecessary struggles**. For instance, if organization isn't your strong suit, you might choose to avoid roles that demand meticulous planning and structure.
- **Find practical workarounds**. Instead of pushing yourself to master an area that doesn't come naturally, you can create

supportive systems, use helpful tools, or seek assistance from others who complement your skill set.

When you truly understand both your strengths and your limitations, you gain clarity about what environments, opportunities, and people bring out the best in you. This self-awareness becomes your compass; it points you toward decisions that resonate with your values, highlight your passions, and align with your natural abilities.

Instead of chasing paths shaped by others' expectations, you begin to carve your own, choosing careers, hobbies, and relationships that reflect who you are. This is the foundation of living with authenticity and creating a life that feels both fulfilling and true.

Identify Core Values and Beliefs

Your core values and beliefs are like a personal compass; guiding how you see the world, make decisions, and build relationships. These inner principles shape the way you live and form the foundation of who you are. Think of your values as the unique tone your instrument adds to the orchestra of life - they give you purpose, direction, and a presence that's uniquely yours.

What Are Core Values?

Core values are the deeply rooted beliefs that reflect what matters most to you. They influence your decisions, shape your relationships, and help you determine what's right and meaningful in your life. Values can be emotional (like kindness or empathy), intellectual (like curiosity or growth), or social (like fairness or responsibility).

Whether your top values include honesty, creativity, freedom, or personal growth, what matters most is that they resonate with who you truly are, not who others expect you to be.

What Are Beliefs?

Beliefs are the assumptions or perceptions you hold about yourself, others, and the world. They shape how you interpret situations and how you respond to them.

Together, your values and beliefs form the "why" behind your actions. While values define what truly matters to you, beliefs influence how you see yourself and what you believe is possible. These internal systems offer clarity, direction, and meaning as you move through life's decisions.

Discovering Your Core Values

Identifying your values doesn't have to be overwhelming. Here's a simple process to help you start:

- **Reflect on What Matters Most**: Think about times you felt proud, fulfilled, or challenged. What values were being honored or tested?
- **Explore Common Values**: Review values like respect, creativity, adventure, honesty, compassion, or freedom. Highlight the ones that resonate.
- **Narrow Your List**: From those you chose, pick the top five that represent what you stand for.
- **Ask Yourself Why**: Why do these stand out? How have they influenced your choices or helped in difficult situations?

By identifying and understanding your values, you gain a clear sense of what drives you. These values become your anchor during times of change or challenge. They help you stay true to yourself and make decisions that feel not only smart but meaningful and aligned with who you are.

When your actions align with your values, you feel more grounded, focused, and fulfilled. There's a deep sense of purpose that comes from knowing your choices reflect the kind of person you want to be. This alignment doesn't just benefit you—it also strengthens your relationships. Others can sense your authenticity and trust you more because your principles consistently show up in what you do.

Take some time to reflect on your values and beliefs. Write them down. Explore why they matter to you. Consider the moments in life when you felt proud or disappointed. What values were present or missing in those moments? When you understand your "why," navigating the "how" and "what" becomes much clearer. Life feels less like a guessing game and more like a path you're choosing intentionally.

Find Your Passion and Motivation

One of the most common questions I get is: "How do I find my passion?" It sounds like a big, life-changing quest - and it is - but not in the magical, one-day revelation kind of way. Finding your passion is a journey of reflection and exploration. It's about paying attention to what energizes you and what matters most.

Passion is like fuel. It gives your goals energy and your actions purpose. It's more than a casual interest. It's that deep sense of enthusiasm or meaningful connection that pulls you toward something with joy and persistence. When you're passionate about something, challenges become stepping stones, and time seems to fly. It feels less like work and more like purpose in motion.

What Is Passion?

Passion is more than simply liking something; it's about feeling deeply connected to an activity, task, or purpose. It's the spark that fuels excitement, energy, and a sense of fulfilment. When you're passionate about something, engaging with it doesn't just feel good; it feels meaningful. It becomes part of your identity, something that energizes you and gives your actions purpose.

But let's be real: passion doesn't make the journey effortless. Challenges, setbacks, and hard work are still part of the process. The difference is that passion gives you the motivation to keep going. It builds your resilience and pushes you to keep showing up even when it's tough, because what you're working toward feels truly worth it.

Uncovering Your Passion

So, how do you find that thing that lights you up inside? Passion isn't always obvious, and discovering it doesn't happen overnight. But with curiosity and reflection, you can begin to uncover what truly drives you.

- **Reflect on What Excites You**: Think about the activities that make you lose track of time or spark joy. What topics or hobbies do you find yourself coming back to again and again? What have you always been curious about or eager to learn?

  For example, do you light up when you're helping others? Do you feel most alive when you're creating something, like writing, painting, or building? These clues matter. The things you're naturally drawn to are often rooted in deeper values and interests.

Consider Your Values. Think about what matters most to you—creativity, community, growth, helping others, or making a difference. When your passions connect with your values, they feel more fulfilling and deeply rooted in who you are.

Experiment and Explore

Passion isn't always something you know right away. Sometimes, you discover it by exploring; trying new things, joining a group, taking a class, or volunteering in areas that spark your curiosity. Exploration gives you the chance to stumble upon something that unexpectedly lights you up.

When you're passionate about something, you feel more connected, more driven, and more alive. It motivates you to push through challenges and keep improving, because the journey matters just as much as the outcome.

Finding your passion isn't about reaching a final destination, it's about the ongoing process of discovery. Along the way, you'll uncover new aspects of yourself, encounter unexpected opportunities, and grow in powerful ways. Passion becomes the energy behind your progress. Whether it shows up in your work, a hobby, or a cause you care deeply about, pursuing it brings more purpose, color, and joy into your life.

So, what's one thing you've always been curious to try? That could be where your passion begins.

Practice and Sharpen Your Skills

Progress isn't about reaching a final destination—it's a journey of steady, intentional movement. Each small step brings you closer to mastering your own unique symphony: a harmonious blend of your talents, values, and aspirations. Like music, mastery takes time, attention, and practice. It's a lifelong pursuit that requires focus, resilience, and a willingness to keep evolving.

To build personal mastery, it helps to focus on a few key areas that work together to support consistent growth:

- **Building Skills and Competencies**: Progress begins with learning. Whether you're developing a technical ability, strengthening your communication, or deepening emotional intelligence, every skill you sharpen adds to your personal toolbox.

Let's look at what this looks like in practice.

Example: Think of a writer refining their craft. Through regular storytelling, editing, and engaging with readers, they not only improve their language but also grow more confident in their voice and purpose. That confidence translates into impact - and impact is the result of practiced skill.

Overcoming Challenges

Growth often comes through resistance. When you face and conquer challenges, you build resilience, sharpen your problem-solving skills, and discover new layers of strength within yourself. Every obstacle is a test - and a teacher.

Example: A marathon runner doesn't stop when fatigue sets in. Instead, they press on, learning how to pace themselves, manage pain, and push past mental barriers. That perseverance not only helps them finish the race but also prepares them for every challenge that follows.

Obstacles may be uncomfortable, but they often hold the key to our next level of growth. The process of overcoming them reveals what we're capable of when we choose persistence over perfection.

Cultivating Habits and Discipline

Success doesn't rely on bursts of motivation, it's built on what you do consistently. The habits you develop and the discipline you maintain are the quiet forces behind every long-term achievement.

Establish routines that serve your goals. Set clear intentions. And most importantly, show up even when you don't feel like it. That's where real progress begins.

Example: A musician doesn't master their instrument by waiting for inspiration. They commit to daily practice, even on tough days. Over time, that discipline becomes second nature, and the music gets better.

Want to stay consistent? Start small: pick one habit that supports your growth and do it daily. Let progress - not perfection - be your focus.

It's easy to fall into the trap of chasing perfection. But the truth is, perfection isn't the goal - **progress** is. Each step forward, no matter how small, is meaningful. Every bit of effort adds to your growth and nudges you closer to your vision.

Progress teaches us to value the journey. It's in the trying, the learning, and the small wins that fulfilment takes root. Mistakes and setbacks aren't signs of failure - they're lessons. Each one refines your path, strengthens your character, and teaches you more about who you are becoming.

Mastering your unique symphony means finding harmony between your talents, your dreams, and the consistent actions you take. Just like in music, where every note - sharp or flat - plays a role in creating something beautiful, every action you take contributes to the masterpiece of your life.

And your symphony doesn't have to sound like anyone else's. That's the point. The beauty lies in its originality, in the blend of your rhythm, your pace, your story.

So, embrace the journey. Celebrate every step - especially the imperfect ones - and trust that each one brings you closer to becoming who you're meant to be. Growth isn't measured in leaps, but in the courage to keep going.

Because in the end, it's not just about where you're going. It's about who you become along the way and how beautifully you learn to play your song.

Overcoming Challenges & Embracing Growth

Every journey of self-improvement comes with its own set of hurdles - just like a powerful musical piece includes difficult passages. These moments test your patience and persistence, but they also present something invaluable: an invitation to grow.

Yes, challenges can be frustrating. They can throw you off rhythm and make you question your ability. But they are also the very experiences that sharpen your resilience, deepen your character, and strengthen your belief in yourself. The key is to shift your perspective - see the difficulties not as stop signs but as stepping stones.

Think of someone learning a new language. At first, it feels clumsy; mispronunciations, grammar confusion, moments of doubt. Mistakes are frequent. But with every stumble, there's a lesson. With every correction, progress is made. Slowly but surely, confidence builds, and fluency emerges.

It's the same with any challenge you face in life. Progress doesn't come from avoiding mistakes—it comes from engaging with them, learning from them, and trying again.

Here are a few strategies to help you navigate challenges with intention and strength:

- **Shift Your Mindset:** Failure isn't the end - it's feedback. When something doesn't go as planned, ask yourself: *What is this teaching me?* Reframing setbacks as opportunities allows you to stay motivated and flexible rather than discouraged.
- **Break It Down:** Big challenges can feel overwhelming, but you don't have to take them on all at once. Break them into smaller, manageable steps. Tackling one piece at a time builds momentum and makes progress feel more achievable.
- **Celebrate Progress, Not Perfection:** It's natural to focus on how far you still have to go, but don't lose sight of how far you've already come. Growth isn't about being flawless; it's about becoming better, one step at a time. Every effort counts.
- **Surround Yourself with Positivity:** The people and energy around you matter more than you think. Seek support from friends, mentors, or even stories of people who've walked a similar path. Their positivity and encouragement can be a powerful motivator when things get tough.

Remember, the goal isn't to avoid obstacles, it's to move through them with awareness and intention. Your setbacks, struggles, and small wins aren't distractions from the journey, they *are* the journey. They're the notes that, together, create your symphony of growth.

Discipline

> *"Discipline is the path between your dreams and your achievements."*

Discipline is a choice, a personal commitment to lead yourself by building a system and sticking to it. It's not about being forced by outside rules. It's about taking ownership of your goals and committing to steady, intentional effort. Discipline provides the structure needed to transform your ambitions into reality.

It isn't about being perfect. It's about showing up - day after day - and taking the next step. Even when motivation runs low, discipline keeps you grounded. It fuels self-control, sharpens focus, and strengthens determination. Without it, even the best intentions can fade.

At its heart, discipline is about forming habits that align with your values and goals. These routines help you stay focused and make progress feel more natural over time. Discipline isn't just a tool, it's a lifestyle that leads to lasting change.

Consistency: The Secret Ingredient

Consistency is the backbone of discipline. Whether you're learning a new skill, developing healthier habits, or chasing a life goal, steady effort is what propels you forward. It's not the intensity of your effort once in a while, it's the small steps repeated daily that create meaningful transformation.

Think of a musician practicing their scales every day. It may not seem exciting, but this steady repetition builds their foundation, sharpens their skills, and prepares them to perform with confidence and expression. Over time, that daily discipline transforms into something powerful - music that moves people.

In the same way, when we stick to our daily habits, we build momentum that moves us closer to our goals. Habits simplify the path to progress. Once a routine is established, it minimizes the need for constant decision-making. Instead of debating whether to take action, your habits step in automatically, reducing resistance and making growth feel more natural.

Discipline helps you:
- **Stay Focused on Your Goals**: It keeps you aligned with your vision, even when life gets distracting.
- **Build Momentum**: Every consistent step adds up, creating a ripple effect of continuous progress.
- **Overcome Obstacles**: It strengthens your resilience and helps you push through challenges with purpose.
- **Achieve Long-Term Success**: The disciplined choices you make today lay the groundwork for the future you envision.

Managing Expectations
The Balance Between Hope and Reality

We all carry expectations of ourselves, of others, and of the world around us. These expectations often act as a guiding light, helping us aim higher and pursue our goals. When aligned with reality, they motivate us and give direction to our dreams.

But expectations can also be a double-edged sword. When they're unrealistic, rigid, or unspoken, they can quietly lead to stress, disappointment, or strained relationships. Learning to manage them thoughtfully is a powerful step toward personal growth and emotional balance.

The Challenges of Unmanaged Expectations

Expectations offer purpose, but when left unchecked, they can create internal and external conflict. Here are some common challenges:

- **Disappointment**: When our expectations don't match reality, it's easy to feel disheartened; sometimes even like we've failed. For instance, expecting to master a new skill in just one week can lead to discouragement if progress is slower than imagined.
- **Unrealistic Standards**: Holding yourself to impossible ideals can breed self-doubt and unnecessary pressure. Even when you're making real progress, you may feel like it's never enough. This mindset erodes confidence and creates a sense of chronic dissatisfaction.

- **Tense Relationships**: Unspoken expectations in relationships often lead to misunderstanding and emotional distance. For instance, expecting a friend to always check in without expressing that need can cause disappointment and resentment for both parties.
- **Overlooking the Present**: When you're constantly focused on future outcomes, it's easy to miss the value of what's happening right now. This mindset can make life feel like a never-ending pursuit rather than something to be experienced and appreciated.
- **Fear of Failure**: When your self-worth becomes tied to achieving specific outcomes, the fear of falling short can become overwhelming. This fear may prevent you from taking chances or stepping outside your comfort zone.
- **Limited Flexibility**: Life is full of unexpected twists. When expectations are rigid, it becomes harder to adjust to change or recognize new opportunities when they appear.
- **Emotional Stress**: Unrealistic or unmet expectations can create a heavy emotional burden. You might feel anxious, disappointed, or even question your worth, all of which can impact your well-being.
- **Low Motivation**: Sometimes, expectations that are too ambitious or poorly defined can actually demotivate rather than

inspire. Instead of feeling driven, you may feel paralyzed or unsure where to start.

- **Pressure on Others**: Expecting others to meet your unspoken needs—such as assuming a partner should "just know" what you want—can place unnecessary strain on relationships and lead to communication breakdowns.

How to Manage Expectations Effectively

Managing expectations is not about lowering your standards, it's about setting yourself up for success. After all, the way we handle our expectations can either drive our progress or drain our energy.

Expectations are a natural part of life, but their impact depends on how we frame and adjust them. When expectations are clear, realistic, and flexible, they become tools for clarity, motivation, and growth rather than triggers for frustration or stress.

Whether you're navigating personal relationships, striving toward career goals, or working on self-improvement, learning to manage expectations helps you stay grounded and centered. It encourages better communication, reduces unnecessary pressure, and allows space for compassion, both for yourself and others.

The goal isn't to dream smaller, but to bring your hopes in line with reality so you can move forward with greater intention, resilience, and peace of mind.

We Are Perfectly Imperfect

In a world that constantly urges us to chase flawlessness, it's easy to forget a powerful truth: *we are perfectly imperfect*. And that's not just acceptable - it's beautiful.

Perfection isn't just unattainable; it's unnecessary. Our quirks, flaws, and missteps are what make us human, relatable, and uniquely shaped by our experiences. To be perfectly imperfect is to live with grace, self-awareness, and openness to growth.

Imagine a life with no struggles, no mistakes, and no rough edges. It might sound ideal at first, but without those imperfections, there would be no creativity, no resilience, and no story worth telling. Challenges give life texture. They teach us what strength looks like in motion, not in stillness. Think about the times you've grown the most; chances are, they began with something that didn't go as planned.

Embracing imperfection isn't just about accepting yourself—it's about recognizing and honoring the humanity in others. Our differences don't divide us; they enrich us.

You don't need to be flawless to be fulfilled. You need to be real, evolving, and kind to yourself along the way. So, let go of perfection. Choose growth, authenticity, and progress instead. That's where true beauty lives.

We Are the Outcome of Our Choices

Who we are today, the life we're living, the progress we've made, and even the challenges we face is shaped largely by the choices we've made along the way. While we can't control every curve life throws at us, we always have the power to decide how we respond.

It's tempting to blame circumstances, other people, or timing when things don't unfold as we hoped. But lasting growth begins when we stop pointing outward and start looking inward. Every decision - big or small - offers insight. Sometimes it shows us what works; other times, it teaches us what to avoid. Even missteps have value when we pause to reflect and adjust.

When we take responsibility for our actions, we reclaim our power. Instead of dwelling on what we can't change, we start focusing on what we can influence: our next step. And in doing so, we move forward - not perfectly, but intentionally - toward a life shaped by purpose and personal truth.

The Power of Value-Based Choices

The choices we make should reflect what we truly value. Whether it's family, personal growth, financial stability, or creativity, aligning our decisions with our core values helps us build a life that feels authentic and meaningful.

Over time, these choices come together like pieces of a mosaic, shaping a vivid picture of who we are and what we stand for. Each decision becomes a small but powerful stroke in the masterpiece of our lives.

And here's the truth: it's never too late to adjust the picture. If our present reflects the sum of past decisions, then every new choice is a chance to reshape our future.

Pause and reflect:
- Are my choices aligned with my goals and values?
- Am I moving closer to the life I want to live?
- What lessons from past decisions can guide my next steps?

By taking the time to reflect and realign, we gain the clarity and strength to make decisions that honour who we are and lead us toward a future that feels purposeful, not accidental.

> *We have the absolute freedom to make choices but have no control over the consequences.*

We are free to make our own choices, but once a choice is made, its consequences unfold beyond our control. This truth can feel overwhelming, yet it's also deeply liberating. It reminds us to choose intentionally, knowing our decisions carry weight and create ripples beyond the moment.

Even when things don't go as planned, the act of choosing remains powerful. Each decision is proof that we are engaged in shaping our journey, not merely drifting, but directing.

Our current reality isn't just shaped by chance; it's a reflection of the paths we've taken. Every decision - whether big or small - has helped bring us to this point. And that's not a burden; it's a gift.

So as you move forward, remember it's not about being flawless, it's about being aligned. Making decisions that honour your values and lead you closer to the life you truly want.

Every choice matters. Every step counts.

Understanding the Stages of Personal Growth

Growth is an unfolding journey, marked by stages that shape who we become. One way to understand these stages is through a model often used in team development: *Forming, Storming, Norming, and Performing.* While created to describe how teams evolve, this framework mirrors the personal evolution we all go through as we navigate challenges, build new habits, and uncover our purpose.

Each season of life brings fresh lessons, new responsibilities, and deeper layers of self-discovery. By recognizing where we are in our own development, we can move forward with greater clarity, patience, and purpose.

As we walk through these stages, you'll begin to see that personal growth isn't linear. It's a rhythm of breakdowns and breakthroughs. And knowing which stage you're in can help you make intentional choices that shape a life of growth and meaning.

Forming: The Foundation of Childhood

In the journey of personal growth, childhood represents the *Forming* stage; a season of curiosity, exploration, and emotional imprinting. This is when we begin building the foundation of who we are, shaped by our earliest experiences and environments.

At this stage, children rely heavily on parents, caregivers, and teachers to help them make sense of the world. They absorb behaviours, beliefs, and emotions through observation and interaction. New experiences - whether exciting, confusing, or challenging - begin to shape their developing sense of identity.

This is also the time when core values begin to take root, and emotional templates for trust, love, and safety are established. The lessons learned here - both spoken and unspoken - often echo throughout life, influencing how we relate to ourselves and others as we grow.

Role of Parents and Caregivers in the Forming Stage
- *Provide a safe and nurturing environment that encourages exploration*
- *Model positive behaviors and respectful communication*
- *Encourage curiosity while establishing clear, healthy boundaries*
- *consistent emotional support to help build confidence and self-esteem*

The Forming stage isn't about perfection; it's about laying a loving, supportive foundation. These early years set the stage for how we learn, how we cope, and how we begin to discover the person we're becoming.

Storming: The Turbulence of Adolescence

The teenage years usher in the *Storming* stage; a powerful mix of emotional highs, identity exploration, and the growing desire for independence. Like a storm rolling through once-calm skies, adolescence can be chaotic, unpredictable, and deeply transformative.

This is a time when teens begin questioning authority, defining their values, and wrestling with peer pressure. Emotions run deep. Choices feel bigger. And underneath it all is a longing to be seen, understood, and accepted on their own terms.

Teenagers may swing between childhood dependence and an urgent pull toward autonomy. They might resist advice but still crave connection and guidance. During this time, they begin making decisions that shape their future; like who they trust, how they define success, and what kind of person they want to become.

Role of Parents and Mentors in the Storming Stage
- *Practice open communication without being controlling*
- *Provide guidance while allowing space for independence*
- *Support them in understanding the consequences of their choices*
- *Be a calm, consistent source of encouragement and reassurance*

The Storming stage can be intense, but it's also necessary.

When met with patience and trust, it becomes a vital bridge from childhood into the fuller discovery of one's unique voice and identity.

Norming: Self-Discovering Young Adulthood

Young adulthood marks the *Norming* stage, a time when individuals begin translating their dreams into deliberate action. It's a season of self-definition, where aspirations are tested against reality, and emerging adults start building the foundation for a life of purpose and independence.

This phase is marked by increasing confidence, active goal setting, and the pursuit of personal and professional stability. As priorities shift, decisions carry more long-term weight, whether it's choosing a career path, committing to a relationship, or setting financial goals.

During this stage, individuals refine their values, build meaningful social and professional connections, and embrace growing responsibility. As they explore what purpose means on their terms, they begin forming the habits, boundaries, and mindsets that support their evolving identity.

Role of Parents and Mentors in the Norming Stage
- Transition from authority figures to trusted mentors
- Support independence while offering emotional and practical guidance
- Encourage self-reflection, goal setting, and long-term vision
- Celebrate milestones to reinforce progress and motivation

Norming is where confidence begins to deepen, and self-identity takes more permanent shape. Though the journey ahead may still have questions, young adults begin to trust in their ability to choose, adapt, and lead themselves forward.

Performing: The Mastery of Mature Adulthood

Mature adulthood marks the *Performing* stage; the point where individuals bring together the lessons of earlier phases to lead with confidence, wisdom, and purpose. This is a season of alignment, where values, skills, and intentions intersect to shape not only personal success but also meaningful contributions to others.

At this stage, many excel in their careers, nurture strong relationships, and give back to their communities. They often step into mentorship roles, guiding others with the insight they've gained over time. Productivity may peak, but the deeper shift is internal toward self-awareness, impact, and legacy.

Still, challenges persist. Whether navigating changes in health, identity, or roles within family and society, growth doesn't stop. In fact, it deepens. Many in this phase seek fulfillment not just in achievement, but in significance; using their experiences to inspire, empower, and uplift those around them.

Role of Parents in the Performing Stage
- Shift into a supportive, advisory role
- Celebrate the independence and accomplishments of their children
- Foster mutual respect and open communication
- Offer perspective and encouragement during times of change or transition

Life doesn't follow a straight path. Each new chapter - moving to a different country, launching a second career, becoming a grandparent - can return us to the *Forming* stage, where learning and adjustment begin anew.

These phases aren't a ladder, but a cycle. Every transition brings its own lessons, every stage its own wisdom. By recognizing where we are and embracing the growth it invites, we move forward with greater clarity, resilience, and grace.

The Evolving Role of Parents

Parenting is not a fixed role, it's a journey of growth, transformation, and love. As children grow and change, so do the responsibilities and rhythms of parenthood. From nurturing early curiosity to guiding the path toward independence, parents evolve alongside their children, offering support and wisdom at every stage.

Every developmental phase brings its own mix of challenges and opportunities. When parents stay flexible, present, and empathetic, they empower their children to navigate transitions with confidence and resilience.

Parents as First Teachers

From day one, parents are a child's first and most influential teachers. In everyday moments - story time, shared meals, answered questions - they lay the foundation for lifelong learning. Through modelling behaviour, encouraging curiosity, and offering a safe space for mistakes, they help children build the confidence to explore and grow.

As children mature, the parental role shifts from instructor to guide. The goal becomes less about providing immediate answers and more about nurturing problem-solving, emotional awareness, and independent thinking. It's not about having all the solutions, it's about empowering children to seek them with confidence.

How Parents Foster Intellectual Growth

Parents play a powerful role in shaping their children's intellectual development. Encouraging exploration, asking thoughtful questions, and providing meaningful challenges helps children build critical thinking, creativity, and confidence.

Here are simple, everyday ways parents can nurture a child's intellectual growth:

- **Encourage curiosity**: Answer their questions patiently, spark conversations, and expose them to a variety of books, places, and ideas.
- **Support independent thinking**: Let children make age-appropriate choices and solve small problems on their own.
- **Provide hands-on learning**: If a child shows interest in something (like building), offer materials such as blocks, kits, or craft supplies to encourage exploration.
- **Allow decision-making**: Give them opportunities to choose their own outfits, plan their lunch, or manage a small allowance. These build confidence and decision-making skills.
- **Teach problem-solving**: Involve them in daily tasks like fixing something broken, preparing a meal, or planning a weekend activity.

- **Assign responsibilities**: Age-appropriate chores like watering plants, setting the table, or making their bed teach accountability and contribution.
- **Encourage stepping out of comfort zones**: Motivate them to try new hobbies, join groups, or take small risks to build adaptability and resilience.
- **Normalize failure as part of learning**: Let children experience setbacks and mistakes without fear. Encourage them to reflect on what they learned and remind them that failure is part of growth.
- **Praise efforts, not just results**: Recognize their creativity, planning, persistence, and courage rather than just the final outcome.

By fostering intellectual curiosity and independence, parents equip their children with critical thinking skills that serve them for life.

Building a Secure Foundation

A child's emotional well-being is deeply connected to the environment their parents create. Emotional security is essential for developing confidence, resilience, and a positive self-image. By modelling empathy, patience, and open communication, parents create a home where children feel safe, valued, and empowered to face life's uncertainties.

Instilling Values & Ethics

Beyond academic and emotional development, parents also play a fundamental role in shaping their children's values and moral compass. Through daily actions, conversations, and guidance, they model integrity, empathy, fairness, and responsibility. Children learn to treat others with respect and to make decisions rooted in their own core values.

Supporting Health & Well-Being

Physical and mental health are pillars of a child's overall development. Parents can lay a strong foundation by encouraging healthy habits from an early age; nutritious eating, regular physical activity, sufficient rest, and open conversations about emotional well-being.

By prioritizing health, parents help children build the energy, focus, and resilience they need to explore their passions and face life's challenges.

Encouraging Independence & Accountability

As children grow, they need space to develop autonomy, make decisions, and take responsibility for their actions. Encouraging independence is a gradual process that prepares them for adulthood. This evolution—from dependence to self-reliance—builds confidence, strengthens resilience, and helps children face the complexities of life with courage and clarity.

Parenting is not a one-size-fits-all journey. Each stage brings its own challenges, requiring patience, creativity, and adaptability. Balancing work and family, managing behaviour shifts, and navigating generational differences can be demanding. But within these challenges are countless moments of joy and connection. Each milestone, from a child's first steps to their first independent decision, reflects a parent's love, presence, and influence. The parenting journey may be complex, but its rewards are deep, lasting, and life-changing—for both parent and child.

When we nurture the mind, body, and spirit, and empower growth through love and guidance, we help our children - and ourselves - lead effective, productive, and purpose-driven lives.

Managing Desires

Desires are powerful internal impulses that move us toward what we want or believe we need. They may stem from emotional, physical, or psychological needs, ranging from basic survival instincts like hunger and shelter to deeper yearnings such as success, connection, or personal validation.

At their core, desires are a natural part of being human. They motivate our actions, influence our decisions, and shape how we invest our time and energy. When in balance, desires can drive growth, spark ambition, and lead to meaningful experiences. But when left unchecked or disconnected from our values, they may foster stress, imbalance, or unhealthy attachments, pulling us away from what truly matters.

Desires become problematic when they override priorities. Chasing fleeting wants without discernment can lead to poor decisions, neglected responsibilities, and a hollow sense of achievement. This is why self-leadership calls for mindful recognition of our desires; pausing to ask: *Does this align with who I am becoming?*

Managing desires isn't about denial. It's about discernment. When desires are aligned with long-term vision and core values, they act as fuel for purpose - not distraction. And that distinction makes all the difference.

When our desires begin to conflict with what truly matters, we often feel a growing sense of inner tension. This imbalance usually surfaces when short-term wants - like recognition, wealth, or status - overshadow the deeper values that ground us: love, purpose, health, and growth.

The pursuit of success or material gain can offer temporary satisfaction, but if these desires become the center of gravity in our lives, they risk hollowing out the very meaning we crave. A life driven by unchecked desire may look polished on the outside yet feel aimless or lonely within.

The irony is that those most driven by external achievement often find that each victory fades quickly, replaced by the pressure to chase the next. The satisfaction is short-lived. The hunger remains.

How to Deal with Desires

To navigate this, we must return to what truly matters; those enduring, quiet truths that give life its depth: connection, integrity, health, and growth. When we center ourselves in these values, desires become companions to purpose, not distractions from it.

But managing desire isn't just a personal task, it's relational, too. In families, workplaces, or teams, we rely on each other. When personal ambition starts to outweigh collective responsibility, it can disrupt trust, slow progress, and erode shared purpose. Harmony within a group is built on balancing individual aspirations with communal well-being.

When personal desires begin to outweigh group responsibilities, they often cause disruptions that go far beyond the individual. Here are a few ways this can unfold:

- **Lack of Cooperation:** When individuals place personal gain - like individual recognition or ambition - above collective goals, it can fracture group cohesion. Members may stop collaborating, working instead in silos or even competing, which derails shared progress.

- **Resentment and Conflict:** If one person's desires consistently interfere with the group's mission, others may begin to feel taken advantage of. Tensions build, trust erodes, and a once unified team can slowly dissolve into division and blame.

- **Inequity:** Unchecked personal ambition can leave others shouldering uneven workloads, especially when tasks are unfairly distributed. This sense of imbalance fosters frustration, lowers morale, and may cause capable members to disengage entirely.

- **Decreased Productivity:** In interdependent settings, productivity relies on shared momentum. When personal desires take precedence over the collective mission, performance begins to suffer. This breakdown is especially damaging when one person's success hinges on the coordinated efforts of the whole group.

- **Loss of Shared Vision:** When individual desires overshadow the group's mission, the collective vision begins to fracture. Over time, members may lose sight of their common purpose, drifting in different directions and undermining the very foundation of the group.

Balancing Personal Desires and Interdependence

For a group to thrive, personal ambitions must be balanced with a commitment to shared responsibilities. This balance doesn't require the sacrifice of personal desires, but rather their integration into the group's larger purpose.

Shared Accountability:

Managing desires in alignment with group values requires mindful self-awareness. It means recognizing that true fulfillment often comes not just from achieving personal goals, but from contributing meaningfully to something larger than oneself.

In collaborative or interdependent environments, group goals and responsibilities often take precedence. Still, this doesn't mean personal desires are ignored; they should be thoughtfully considered, communicated, and aligned with shared objectives.

However, there are moments when personal needs must come first, particularly in times of crisis or urgent challenges that affect one's health or well-being. In such instances, group flexibility and empathy are vital. The collective must be willing to adjust temporarily to support the individual, trusting that mutual respect and understanding ultimately strengthen the group.

Instant Gratification

Instant gratification is the urge to seek immediate pleasure or reward, often at the cost of long-term fulfillment. It's the choice to prioritize short-term satisfaction, like scrolling through social media instead of working on a meaningful task or reaching for junk food despite health goals. While these moments of indulgence can offer brief comfort or distraction, unchecked gratification may slowly undermine discipline, long-term goals, and personal growth. The ability to delay gratification is not about denying joy, it's about aligning short-term actions with long-term values.

Attitude - *A Double-Edged Sword*

Attitude isn't just a mindset, it's a dynamic force that shapes how we experience the world. Like a double-edged sword, it can empower us or limit us. When positive, attitude becomes a driver of resilience, creativity, and forward movement. When negative, it can reinforce helplessness, resistance to change, or even bitterness. Understanding and consciously adjusting our attitude is key to navigating both internal and external challenges effectively.

The Foundation of Attitude: Paradigm

Beneath attitude lies paradigm; the lens through which we interpret life. This framework of beliefs, assumptions, and perspectives informs how we perceive situations, people, and ourselves. Paradigm acts like a mental filter, colouring our interpretations and shaping our emotional and behavioural responses. Because of this deep interconnection, a shift in paradigm can transform attitude. Changing how we *see* often changes how we *respond* - making paradigm work a vital part of emotional growth.

How Paradigm Shapes Attitude

Our paradigm deeply influences our attitude.
- A growth-oriented paradigm encourages optimism, a love for learning, and perseverance.
- A fixed or limiting paradigm breeds resistance, self-doubt, and negativity.

For instance, someone who believes that failure is a stepping stone to growth is likely to respond to setbacks with motivation and curiosity. In contrast, someone who sees failure as a reflection of their worth may feel fear, frustration, or defeat when facing challenges.

The way we think (our paradigm) fuels how we feel and act (our attitude). Together, they create a feedback loop that continuously shapes our behaviours and experiences. A positive paradigm inspires a proactive attitude, which leads to wiser decisions and healthier outcomes. A limiting paradigm, however, tends to reinforce a narrow attitude that may increase stress, close off opportunities, and strain relationships.

The encouraging truth is this: we are not stuck with the paradigms and attitudes we've inherited or developed. Both can be reshaped through conscious effort, reflection, and learning.

Shifting Your Paradigm to Shape Your Attitude

Because our paradigm influences our attitude, shifting how we see ourselves and the world can lead to meaningful and lasting change.

- **Challenge Limiting Beliefs**: Notice where you're holding yourself back and begin to reframe those beliefs into empowering possibilities.

- **Cultivate Self-Awareness**: Observe your thought patterns and how they influence your emotional responses and decisions.
- **Practice Gratitude**: Directing your focus toward what's working can reshape your perspective and energize a more constructive attitude.
- **Surround Yourself with Positivity**: People and environments impact mindset; choose relationships and settings that uplift and support growth.
- **Adopt a Learning Mindset**: View challenges not as threats but as opportunities to evolve, adapt, and become more resilient.

Shifting your paradigm is not a one-time event but a daily practice. Each effort plants the seed for a mindset that supports long-term growth, confidence, and fulfillment.

Chapter 2

From Independent to Interdependent

Achieving Performance Mastery as Part of a Group

When I first picked up the guitar, I was hooked by the thrill of mastering it on my own. The freedom to improvise, explore different styles, and play at my own pace was exhilarating. There were no rules - just me and the music. Each chord felt like a discovery, and every song was a reflection of my creativity.

But everything changed when I started playing with others. Suddenly, it wasn't just about my rhythm or melody anymore; I had to coordinate with other musicians and instruments. The freedom I once cherished began to feel like a burden. The conductor, waving that tiny baton, seemed like a dictator, controlling every note and movement. I resisted. Why should I follow someone else's timing? Why couldn't I just play my way?

I was frustrated. I felt invisible, like my individual expression was being drowned out by the group's structure. I struggled to find my place.

The Shift to Group Collaboration

Playing in a group demanded a completely different kind of skill. It wasn't just about knowing my part; it was about understanding how my music fit into the bigger picture. I had to listen - really listen - adjust my timing, and find the delicate balance between standing out and blending in. It required patience, humility, coordination, and a lot of practice.

Over time, I began to see things differently. The conductor wasn't there to control us - he was there to guide us. His role was to help each musician bring out their best while ensuring we worked together as a unified team. He was like a lighthouse, steady and clear, keeping us aligned during rehearsals and helping us hit the right notes together.

I realized that playing in an ensemble didn't mean losing my freedom. Instead, it meant becoming part of something bigger - something richer and more beautiful than I ever could've created on my own.

That insight stayed with me.

Years later, I entered the corporate world. I worked in training, consulting, teaching, and leading international teams. And as I advanced in my career, I couldn't help but notice a familiar rhythm beneath it all.

The foundations of teamwork in an office were strikingly similar to those in a music ensemble:

- Every team member has a role to play. Just like in an orchestra, each person brings their own strengths and skills to the performance.
- A great leader is like a conductor. Their job isn't to control - it's to guide, ensuring that every contribution blends into a cohesive outcome.
- Success depends on communication and collaboration. In both music and business, listening is just as important as speaking (or playing).

The stage may have changed, but the lesson remained: harmony is achieved not through individual brilliance alone, but through coordinated effort, shared purpose, and mutual respect.

The Power of Interdependence

Playing music taught me invaluable lessons about teamwork and leadership. It showed me the importance of aligning individual talents with a shared vision, just like musicians harmonize their instruments to create a symphony. These lessons made one truth very clear: true excellence isn't about going solo. It's about coming together to create something extraordinary.

Whether in music or business, the magic happens when independence evolves into interdependence - a space where people retain their individuality while working toward a common goal.

Balancing Personal Mastery and Team Harmony

No matter where you are in life or what you do, you are part of an orchestra. Each of us plays a dual role: sometimes we lead, and sometimes we follow. At times, you're the conductor guiding others; at other times, you're focused on your own performance, influencing and being influenced by those around you.

This balance between self-mastery and team contribution is what creates real harmony - not just in music, but in life.

Personal mastery is the foundation. Whether you're honing your skills, refining your talents, or investing in personal growth, becoming your best self is what enables you to contribute meaningfully to any team. But life rarely unfolds in isolation. You might shine as a solo performer, but true growth often begins when you step into a group and learn to collaborate.

True growth often comes when you transition from working independently to thriving interdependently. This shift isn't just about being around others; it's about building meaningful connections, aligning your efforts with theirs, and contributing to something greater than what you could accomplish on your own. It's the difference between being a soloist and becoming part of an orchestra.

When you perform solo, the focus is solely on you. Your success hinges entirely on your individual execution. But in a team - or an orchestra - everyone's role matters. Success comes from each person being in sync, coordinating their efforts, and blending their strengths to create something truly harmonious.

Interdependence goes beyond simply working beside others. It means embracing collaboration, sharing responsibility, and offering mutual support. It's the understanding that each person contributes something unique, and when those pieces fit together, the result is far more powerful. In a symphony, every musician brings a distinct voice, but it's the conductor who brings clarity, cohesion, and direction to the whole.

A New Mindset

The shift from independence to interdependence requires more than just collaboration; it demands a fundamental change in how we define success. When you're operating independently, success often centers on personal achievement. But when you perform interdependently, success becomes a shared accomplishment. It's not just about what you can do alone, but how your contribution supports a larger goal. Your success is intertwined with the team's success.

When you're interdependent, your focus expands from asking, *"What's my role?"* to *"How does my role support the bigger picture?"*

Key Skills for Interdependence and Group Mastery

Thriving in a group setting means learning how to give your best while creating space for others to do the same.

Some of those key skills are:

- **Communication:** Effective communication is vital in any group dynamic. It ensures clarity, builds trust, and strengthens relationships.
    o Express your ideas in a clear, respectful way; don't assume others think the way you do.
    o Listen actively, with the intention to understand, not just respond.
    o Offer constructive feedback that uplifts, rather than undermines.

Imagine an orchestra. If one musician plays out of sync, the entire performance suffers. In the same way, clear, open communication keeps everyone aligned and in harmony.

- **Alignment:** Interdependence thrives when every team member understands their role and respects the roles of others.
  Think of a sports team. Each player has a specific position, but their success depends on strategic collaboration to achieve the shared goal of winning.

- **Flexibility:** Unlike working solo, being part of a team means adapting to different perspectives, personalities, and unexpected challenges.

Maintaining focus on the bigger picture - and recognizing that the group's goal takes precedence over personal preferences - is what allows teams to stay unified in motion.

Everyone brings unique skills, perspectives, and experiences to the table. These differences, when orchestrated with intention, enhance creativity and lead to stronger, more innovative solutions.

Challenges and Conflicts Are Inevitable

Even the most cohesive teams encounter obstacles. What sets interdependent teams apart is their resilience; their ability to respond to difficulties constructively rather than destructively. Instead of allowing tension to derail progress, they face challenges with emotional maturity and collective responsibility:

- Address issues early and collaboratively.
- Learn and grow from mistakes rather than assigning blame.
- Focus on solutions that benefit the group.
- Keep reminding the team of the impact of their shared efforts.

Shifting to interdependence is not about losing your individuality but contributing your unique strengths to something bigger than yourself. It's a conscious choice to align your personal mastery with a collective goal.

By making this shift, you not only expand your own potential but also help shape something extraordinary. It's a reminder that we are stronger together than we could ever be alone.

Achieving alignment is essential for success in any organization. However, the complexity of this alignment changes depending on whether you're working within your immediate team or coordinating across departments. Both contexts bring different dynamics, much like the difference between jamming in a small band and performing in a full-scale orchestra. Each demands different levels of coordination, awareness, and collaboration, but all depend on shared vision and trust.

Creating alignment within a team requires more than shared purpose; it demands understanding and adaptation across diverse work styles, personalities, and expectations.

However, creating harmony within the team has its own challenges:

- **Misaligned Work Styles**: Team members often approach tasks differently. While some thrive on structure and detailed planning, others prefer flexibility and creativity. These contrasting styles can cause friction or slow progress if the team doesn't find a shared rhythm.
- **Unclear Roles**: Without clearly defined responsibilities, tasks may be duplicated or neglected. This overlap or ambiguity can lead to inefficiencies, misunderstandings, and frustration within the team.
- **Personality Clashes**: Differences in temperament - such as assertiveness versus reservation - can create tension when not

navigated with empathy. Misunderstandings may escalate into conflict, disrupting the team's ability to collaborate smoothly.

- **Communication Breakdowns**: Even within small teams, misunderstandings happen. Assumptions, unclear instructions, and lack of feedback can all disrupt collaboration, leading to missed deadlines, subpar work, and growing frustration.
- **Conflicting Priorities**: Individual team members may pursue personal goals that conflict with collective objectives. This misalignment can create internal competition, disengagement, or tension that undermines team performance.

Overcoming barriers to team alignment starts with intentional actions.

The following are ways to build a stronger sense of unity and collaboration:

As a team member:

- **Improve Communication Skills:**
    - Practice active listening to fully understand others.
    - Address misunderstandings quickly and respectfully.
    - Keep communication clear, timely, and transparent.
- **Build Trust and Respect:**
    - Show empathy and take time to understand your teammates' perspectives.
    - Support others and foster a culture of mutual respect.
    - Be reliable and follow through on your commitments.

- **Clarify Roles and Expectations:**
    - Openly discuss and agree on each person's responsibilities.
    - Understand how your role impacts others, and how their roles impact you.
- **Be Open to Feedback:**
    - Seek constructive feedback and accept it as a tool for growth.
    - Encourage open dialogue and remain receptive, not defensive.
    - Reflect on input and use it to improve your approach and contribution.
- **Focus on Shared Goals:**
    - Revisit the team's objectives regularly to stay aligned and motivated.
- **Adapt and Be Flexible:**
    - Adjust your working style when needed to support the team's rhythm.
    - Embrace change and collaborate on new solutions together.
- **Address Conflicts Early:**
    - Approach conflicts with calm, respect, and an open mind.
    - Work to find common ground.
    - Keep the focus on the issue, not the person.

- **Strengthen Relationships:**
    - Foster unity through shared goals and trust.
    - Take time to genuinely get to know your teammates.
    - Build rapport through small moments of connection and consistency.
    - Be mindful of how your emotions influence the group dynamic.
- **Stay Organized and Accountable:**
    - Track your tasks, deadlines, and progress regularly.
    - Hold yourself accountable for both individual and team contributions.
    - Maintain clarity in your responsibilities and follow through consistently.

As a team leader:
- Encourage regular check-ins and feedback loops to ensure clarity and cohesion.
- Clearly define each member's role and how their work contributes to the team's vision.
- Invest in team-building activities to foster connection and trust.
- Create a psychologically safe space where ideas are welcomed, not judged.

Collaborating across departments is more complex. Each department functions like a distinct "instrument," with its own rhythm, objectives, and internal culture. Achieving alignment here requires a broader approach, one that values both shared vision and respect for diverse perspectives.

Challenges Facing Alignment

- **Different Objectives and Metrics:** Departments often pursue distinct goals with different success metrics. For instance, the marketing team may focus on brand awareness, while the sales team emphasizes revenue. When these objectives conflict, one department's actions may inadvertently hinder another's progress, leading to tension.

- **Siloed Communication:** Lack of transparency and poor information sharing between departments can delay or distort key messages. When communication breaks down, misunderstandings increase, and collaboration suffers.

- **Competing for Resources:** Departments frequently compete for limited resources; such as budgets, staff, or time. This competition can foster a silo mentality, where teams prioritize their own success over the broader organizational mission.

- **Varied Timelines and Priorities:** Each department often operates on its own schedule. For example, product development may require months to launch a new feature, while customer service needs immediate solutions. These timeline differences can cause dependencies to falter and frustration to mount.

Within a team, the goal is to create harmony among similar players. Across departments, the challenge becomes blending different instruments into a unified symphony. Alignment doesn't happen by accident, it requires conscious effort. By recognizing these unique barriers and adopting thoughtful strategies to overcome them, organizations can foster greater collaboration, spark innovation, and elevate collective performance.

Listening in an Interdependent Environment

As we move from independence to interdependence, one essential skill rises to the forefront: *listening*. This isn't merely about hearing; it's about understanding, aligning, and building trust. In collaborative environments, listening becomes the foundation of effective teamwork, allowing people to connect deeply and work toward shared goals.

What Is Active Listening?

Listening is not passive; it's an engaged process of receiving, interpreting, and responding to information. Active listening goes beyond words; it involves tuning in to the speaker's intent, tone, facial expressions, and body language. It requires empathy, focus, and a willingness to truly absorb the message before reacting or forming judgments.

Just as musicians in an orchestra must listen carefully to one another - and to the conductor - team members must engage in active listening to stay attuned to roles, responsibilities, and the overall rhythm of the group. In music, a single misstep can throw off an entire performance. Similarly, in teams, breakdowns in communication can derail momentum and create misalignment.

When individuals truly listen, they foster connection, prevent misunderstandings, and ensure that every voice contributes to a shared purpose.

Tips for Improving Listening

To sharpen your listening skills, begin by eliminating distractions and giving the speaker your undivided attention. Whether you're in a meeting, a brainstorming session, or a one-on-one conversation, presence is everything. Demonstrate engagement by asking clarifying questions when something isn't clear and reflecting back what you've heard to confirm understanding. For example, saying, *"So what I'm hearing is..."* not only shows attentiveness but also helps prevent miscommunication.

Another effective practice is to summarize or paraphrase key points throughout the conversation. This helps both speaker and listener stay aligned. These small actions build trust and reinforce a sense of respect and collaboration. Ultimately, strong listening creates a space where team members feel seen, heard, and valued; fostering cooperation, trust, and openness.

The Power of Collaboration in Music and Teams

Picture a symphony orchestra preparing to perform. Each musician is a master of their instrument, contributing a distinct sound to the larger composition. But it's not their individual skill that makes the performance soar; it's their ability to listen to each other, to adjust their timing, dynamics, and flow in service of the whole.

The harmony doesn't arise from talent alone. It comes from attention, flexibility, and a shared commitment to something greater than the self.

The same holds true in teams. True success happens when individuals align their strengths with a collective purpose. It's not just about achieving personal milestones; it's about lifting each other up, refining ideas together, and reaching shared goals. Fulfillment comes when you see how your unique contribution enhances the group's efforts and moves the entire vision forward.

Active Listening and Adaptability

Effective teamwork requires both flexibility and attentiveness. In an orchestra, a violinist might soften their playing to let the oboe lead, or a percussionist may shift rhythm in response to the conductor's cues. This kind of dynamic adjustment - guided by active listening - is equally vital in team environments. Being tuned into others' contributions helps maintain balance, fosters collaboration, and allows each member to respond in ways that support the group's collective momentum.

Shifting from Independence to Interdependence

Teamwork demands a shift from solo effort to shared responsibility. It means understanding that personal success is woven into the success of the group. When you value the strengths and contributions of others, you begin to align your goals with the team's broader objectives.

This shift brings deeper fulfillment. In a team, satisfaction often comes not from individual recognition, but from knowing you helped accomplish something greater together.

Even the most accomplished musicians continually refine their performance, just as we can keep growing through our experiences in collaboration. Every challenge becomes an opportunity to improve, not only as individuals, but as teammates. By embracing feedback and finding ways to support the team more effectively, you continue to sharpen your skills and strengthen your role within the group.

Managing Relationships in the Light of Misunderstanding and Conflict

Being part of a group - whether in school, at work, or within families - can bring great joy and a sense of belonging. But it also comes with challenges, especially when relationships are tested by misunderstanding and conflict.

Disagreements often stem from different perspectives, beliefs, and personal histories. These differences can create tension, even when everyone has good intentions. When people view a situation through their own lens, it can lead to miscommunication or emotional distance.

That's why it's so important to pause and try to see things from the other person's point of view. This doesn't mean you have to agree with them, but it does mean you're listening with empathy and respect. With that openness, it becomes easier to navigate disagreement without defensiveness.

Conflict is a natural part of human interaction. What matters is how we respond. Rather than letting it cause division or frustration, we can choose to use it as a doorway to better understanding and stronger connections. Disappointment and differences don't have to end in anger; they can actually pull us closer when handled with maturity and care.

Anger often shows up when reality doesn't match our expectations; whether it's how others behave, how situations unfold, or how we're treated. These gaps between what we hope for and what actually happens can lead to disappointment, frustration, and ultimately, anger.

Recognizing and managing our emotional responses is a powerful skill. It gives us space to respond with thoughtfulness instead of reacting on impulse. In moments of tension, respectful communication becomes essential. Being assertive doesn't mean being aggressive; it means expressing your own needs clearly, without dismissing someone else's.

Choosing to handle differences, disagreements, and disappointments without anger or resentment takes practice and intention. But when you meet conflict with empathy, respect, and a willingness to listen, you open the door to connection and understanding - even when you don't agree.

It Is Not About the *"What"* ... It's About the *"How"*!

The approach, tone, and method of communication often matter more than the issue itself. The *"What"* may represent your intended outcome or the situation or behaviour under consideration. The *"How"* represents the manner in which we act, communicate, engage, and respond. How we express our thoughts and emotions determines whether we build a connection or create conflict. A calm, respectful approach fosters understanding, while a confrontational tone can make things worse.

- *Take a deep breath, pause before responding, and use a calm tone of voice*
- *Give full attention, maintain eye contact, nod, and avoid interrupting*
- *Reflect back what the other person says to confirm understanding*
- *Use open-ended questions that invite further sharing*
- *Recognize emotions without judgment*
- *Be honest about your thoughts, but express them with care*

These same principles apply when working with a team. Knowing your role and how it connects with others is key to harmony and shared success.

To-do list for effective team members:
- Make sure you're well-tuned
- Practice and master your instrument; the role you're assigned to play
- Be very clear on what's expected from you
- Understand how your role contributes to the team's overall goals
- Appreciate how others' roles also drive the team forward
- Recognize how your work both impacts and is impacted by others
- Listen actively and communicate clearly
- Respect and value the strengths of other team members
- Collaborate and stay aligned

When we shift focus from *what* we say or do to *how* we show up, we build bridges instead of walls. That's where true connection begins.

> *"It's not sameness that creates harmony; it's the respectful integration of differences."*

Chapter 3

Lead Like a Maestro

Moving from Follower to Leader

In every orchestra, the maestro stands at the center; focused and fully present. Their task isn't just waving a baton. They interpret a shared vision, coordinate diverse players, and guide the entire performance. A single misstep can throw everything off, but with clarity and grace, the maestro brings harmony from potential chaos.

Great leaders do the same. Much like a maestro, a strong leader aligns individuals with a common goal. They direct efforts, encourage unity, and hold space for each person's unique contribution. Without this sense of direction, even the most skilled team can lose momentum.

- *Leadership is about more than issuing commands*
- *It's about listening, adjusting, and creating cohesion*
- *Vision alone isn't enough; alignment makes the difference*

Beyond vision, coordination becomes essential. Leaders guide in real time, respond to changes, and bring clarity when confusion creeps in. They don't just tell people where to go, they help them find the rhythm to get there together.

The Transformation

Becoming a leader isn't just a change in title, it's a shift in who you are. Moving from follower to leader means stepping into deeper emotional intelligence, sharper communication, and a willingness to serve others through influence rather than control.

- *It requires clarity and courage*
- *It means holding responsibility, not just following instructions*
- *And it often calls for personal growth before positional power*

This transformation is both internal and external. It demands we lead ourselves first before we can lead others well.

The Foundation of Leadership

> *"The ability to guide others begins with the ability to guide yourself."*

Before you can lead others, you must first lead yourself. Self-leadership is the discipline of guiding your own actions, choices, and growth. It's built on a foundation of self-awareness, personal responsibility, and emotional discipline; traits that define strong, lasting leaders.

In a world that shifts constantly, where uncertainty is the norm and complexity the backdrop, self-leadership is no longer optional.

It's essential. It empowers you to adapt with confidence, make sound decisions under pressure, and stay grounded in your values even when things get chaotic. Aspiring leaders must be relentless in their pursuit of growth because the ability to guide others begins with the ability to guide yourself.

Bringing the Vision to Life

Only when you've learned to lead yourself can you begin to lead others with clarity and intention.

A maestro doesn't merely conduct - they elevate. They draw the best from every musician, blending passion with precision to produce something extraordinary. In the same way, great leaders don't just assign tasks or set goals. They empower. They clarify. They cultivate a space where creativity and collaboration flourish.

Vision is only the beginning. To bring it to life, a leader must align efforts, encourage personal ownership, and unify individuals around a shared purpose. Just as a maestro transforms scattered notes into a breathtaking performance, a leader turns strategy into shared success, guiding not by command, but by connection.

Whether you are stepping into leadership for the first time or evolving your style with experience, remember: leadership is not a position, it is a practice, a responsibility, and an art form in motion. Your ability to guide, inspire, and unify others will shape not only your results, but your legacy.

Skills You Need to Shift from a Team Player to a Leader

Transitioning from a team player to a leader requires more than technical expertise; it calls for vision, strategic thinking, and the ability to inspire and align others. An effective leader must guide individuals toward a shared goal while ensuring cohesion and collaboration across the team.

Below are key skills necessary for making this shift successfully:

- **Ability to Interpret the Vision**

A leader's first responsibility is to understand and translate an organization's vision into actionable strategies. This involves breaking down broad objectives into SMART goals so that teams can execute with clarity and direction. Just as a maestro ensures every musician understands their role in a symphony, a leader must communicate expectations clearly, align efforts, and map a path toward the shared goal.

> *Key Action: Clarify individual responsibilities and consistently show team members how their contributions fit into the bigger picture. This fosters purpose and direction across the team.*

- **Understanding Interdependencies**

Strong leaders recognize that departments, roles, and projects do not operate in silos - they are interconnected. By understanding these relationships, leaders can make informed decisions, reduce risks, and allocate resources strategically. When leaders highlight how each function contributes to the organization's broader mission, they inspire collaboration and drive deeper engagement. Employees stop seeing their tasks in isolation and start viewing them as essential parts of a greater whole.

Key Action: Consistently communicate how each team's contributions impact the organization's mission. This reinforces collaboration and fosters cross-functional alignment.

Aligning Performance Across Teams

Leadership isn't about steering a single team, it's about orchestrating alignment across the entire organization. Like a conductor ensuring harmony between different sections of an orchestra, great leaders bring together departments to collaborate, not compete. By aligning performance, leaders increase efficiency, reduce redundancies, and fuel innovation through shared momentum.

Key Action: Define shared objectives and establish KPIs that promote collaboration across teams. This ensures everyone is moving in the same direction with purpose and clarity.

Developing Personal and Group Skills

Once team performance is aligned, effective leaders turn their focus to growing the people who drive those results. Leadership involves not only achieving goals but also developing the individuals and groups who make progress possible. Personal growth builds confidence and capability, while team skills - communication, collaboration, alignment, and problem-solving - create the synergy needed to overcome challenges and adapt to change. A team that develops together performs better under pressure and sustains momentum over time.

    Key Action: *Invest in coaching, training, and mentorship to fuel individual development and strengthen group collaboration.*

℘ Recognizing and Leveraging Individual Talents

Great leaders see beyond job titles; they recognize the unique strengths each person brings to the table. When leaders take the time to identify and activate these talents, they don't just boost engagement; they elevate performance. People are more likely to contribute their best when they feel seen, trusted, and valued. This not only fosters a positive team culture but also encourages innovation, authenticity, and long-term commitment.

    Key Action: *Match roles to individual strengths and celebrate each person's contribution. This builds morale and motivates excellence.*

Fundamentals of Self-Leadership

Before a leader can guide others, they must learn to guide themselves. Self-leadership is the foundation upon which all other forms of leadership are built. It begins within, through introspection, discipline, and purposeful action.

- **Self-Awareness:**

    Self-awareness is the cornerstone of self-leadership. It involves recognizing your emotions, identifying your strengths and weaknesses, and understanding your values and what motivates you. Leaders who are self-aware are better equipped to make thoughtful decisions, manage stress, and lead with authenticity. Start cultivating self-awareness through regular reflection, journaling, or seeking feedback from trusted peers.

- **Personal Responsibility & Accountability:**

    Effective self-leadership demands full ownership of actions and their outcomes. It means acknowledging mistakes, learning from them, and refusing to shift blame. Accountability builds resilience, maturity, and trustworthiness. One powerful method is to write down your goals and identify the specific commitments and deadlines you're holding yourself to. This process reinforces personal follow-through and keeps your intentions visible.

- **Goal Setting:**
  Clear, meaningful goals give self-leadership direction. When aligned with a larger vision, these goals inspire consistency and drive. Effective leaders set goals that are Specific, Measurable, Achievable, Relevant, and Time-bound (SMART). This framework ensures that goals are not only well-defined but also realistic and motivating.

Elements of Self-Leadership

Self-Discipline & Time Management

Self-discipline is the ability to stay committed to your goals, even when faced with distractions or challenges. It fuels consistency and helps maintain momentum. Time management goes hand in hand with discipline, ensuring that your limited hours are spent on what matters most. Leaders who master both are able to stay focused, meet deadlines, and reduce stress caused by procrastination or disorganization.

Prioritize Before You Schedule

Effective leaders don't just manage time—they manage priorities. Prioritizing tasks before scheduling them ensures that your time and energy are devoted to what truly moves the needle. By addressing high-impact tasks first, you avoid the stress of looming deadlines and reduce the mental clutter that comes with juggling too many responsibilities.

Prioritization also keeps your daily actions aligned with long-term goals. It gives you the flexibility to adjust to interruptions without losing focus on what's most important. When your priorities are clear, it becomes easier to reschedule or defer lower-value tasks without compromising your overall progress.

Tips for Setting Your Priorities

To lead yourself effectively, you must evaluate your tasks using clear criteria. Below are key factors that can guide how you prioritize:

- **Urgency**
  - Is there a specific deadline to meet?
  - Will delaying the task create problems, inconvenience, or missed opportunities?

- **Importance**
  - Is the task tied to a long-term goal or strategic objective?
  - Is it a prerequisite for another task or milestone?

- **Impact**
  - How will completing (or delaying) this task affect the overall outcome for the team or project?
  - Are other tasks dependent on the completion of this one?

- **Stakeholder Expectations**

- Is this task a high priority for a manager, client, or colleague?
- Are others waiting on you to move forward?

- **Risk & Consequences**
  - Could delaying this task result in penalties, financial loss, or reputational damage?
  - What's at stake if this task is ignored or postponed?

Decision-Making & Problem Solving

Effective self-leadership involves making thoughtful decisions and solving problems with creativity and confidence. This requires critical thinking, analysis, and the courage to take calculated risks.

Start by weighing the pros and cons of your available options. Consider both short- and long-term consequences. Revisit your SWOT analysis to evaluate each option's strengths, weaknesses, opportunities, and threats. This comprehensive perspective helps you make more informed and confident decisions.

Challenges Facing Self-Leadership

Even strong self-leaders face internal barriers. Procrastination, self-doubt, and fear of failure are common challenges that can derail progress. Overcoming them requires resilience, adaptability, and a growth mindset to stay grounded and forward-moving.

- **Procrastination:**

Self-leadership means staying motivated and disciplined even without external accountability. Procrastination often arises when tasks feel overwhelming, unclear, or uninspiring.

Breaking work into smaller, manageable parts and celebrating small wins can help rebuild momentum.

- **Fear of Failure:**

Failure is not the end - it's feedback. Shift your focus from outcomes to the learning process. Set realistic goals, build gradually, and remind yourself that mistakes are part of growth. Use setbacks as tools to recalibrate and refine your next steps.

- **Seeking Perfection:**

Focus on progress rather than perfection. Mistakes are part of the learning process, not proof of inadequacy. Break tasks into manageable steps and celebrate progress along the way. Often, "good enough" is all that's needed to move forward and achieve meaningful success.

- **Lack of Clarity & Direction:**

When you feel stuck or directionless, reconnect with your "why" - the deeper purpose behind your goal. If you're unsure how to begin, ask for guidance from a mentor, peer, or trusted resource. Take one clear step at a time and reassess regularly to stay aligned. Clarity often emerges through action; so start, even if it's small.

- **Overwhelming Tasks:**

Overwhelm can stall momentum. Break large tasks into smaller, prioritized steps and set realistic deadlines for each. Focus on one step at a time. If possible, delegate responsibilities and ask for help. This structured approach can replace anxiety with a growing sense of accomplishment.

- **Low Motivation:**

When motivation wanes, reconnect with the purpose behind the task. Remind yourself how it aligns with your bigger goals and values. Sometimes, a change of environment or seeking out inspiring content can reignite your enthusiasm and get you moving again.

- **Poor Time Management:**

Time management is a foundational self-leadership skill. Prioritize tasks by importance and urgency, using tools like checklists or digital planners. Break large projects into smaller, time-blocked actions. Minimize distractions and check in with your progress regularly, adjusting your plan when necessary to stay aligned.

- **Distraction:**

In today's world, distractions are constant. Identify your biggest sources of interruption; whether digital, environmental, or emotional, and take proactive steps to reduce them. A distraction-free workspace and clear priorities can significantly boost your focus and overall productivity.

- **Lack of Accountability:**

Without self-accountability, it becomes easy to slip into cycles of procrastination and avoidance. Taking personal ownership of your goals strengthens your sense of control and reinforces commitment. It also reduces stress and builds a stronger connection between your intentions and your actions.

The Art of Leading Others

Leadership is more than a title or position; it's the ability to inspire, influence, and empower others to move collectively toward a shared vision. While self-leadership centers on personal growth, discipline, and internal motivation, leading others demands an outward shift in focus: creating alignment, building relationships, and nurturing a culture where people thrive.

Effective leadership blends vision, communication, trust, and adaptability. It's not about control; it's about creating conditions where teams feel connected to a purpose, encouraged to contribute their strengths, and supported through change.

Inspiring with Vision

Great leaders do more than manage tasks, they inspire people through vision. A compelling vision acts as a guiding light, helping teams stay motivated, even during uncertainty. When individuals understand how their work contributes to something larger, it fuels a sense of purpose and pride.

> ***Tip:*** *Regularly remind team members of the "why" behind their work. Align personal and team goals with the broader mission to keep energy and focus high.*

Building Trust as the Foundation

Trust is the heartbeat of effective leadership. Without it, teams may comply, but they won't commit. When trust is present, individuals feel seen, respected, and safe to take initiative or speak honestly. Leaders build trust not through perfection, but through integrity, empathy, and consistency over time.

> *Tip:* Keep your promises. Be transparent about decisions, especially when facing challenges. Show vulnerability when appropriate—it builds credibility, not weakness.

Leading Through Change with Adaptability

Change is the only constant in leadership. Whether due to market shifts, organizational restructuring, or unforeseen challenges, great leaders must remain grounded under pressure. The ability to adjust strategies while maintaining team morale sets adaptable leaders apart. They don't just survive change, they lead through it.

> *Tip:* Anticipate potential roadblocks, develop flexible strategies, and foster a resilient team culture that embraces growth through uncertainty.

Seeing the Bigger Picture

A great leader, much like a skilled conductor, understands how each individual part contributes to the harmony of the whole. Strategic leadership requires more than focusing on one's own department; it demands awareness of how diverse teams interconnect and influence overall outcomes. This holistic view helps prevent division and encourages collaboration across boundaries.

Tip: Build relationships beyond your immediate team. Understanding how different departments operate enables you to lead with clarity and cohesion.

Cultivating Accountability Through Communication

Leadership isn't just about delegating, it's about guiding, aligning, and communicating effectively. Just as a maestro uses precise gestures to unify an orchestra, leaders must provide clear direction and meaningful feedback. Accountability thrives where expectations are understood and communication flows openly.

Tip: Create space for honest dialogue. Make sure team members feel heard and always connect feedback to shared objectives and progress.

Leadership Styles

One hallmark of effective leadership is adaptability. Situational leadership, developed by Paul Hersey and Ken Blanchard, emphasizes the importance of adjusting one's leadership style based on the team's readiness, experience, and confidence. Rather than relying on a one-size-fits-all approach, leaders assess the needs of each individual or group and respond accordingly.

Among the core leadership styles in this model is Directing, a highly structured and guidance-oriented approach.

Directing

Imagine the first rehearsal of a complex new symphony. The orchestra - composed of seasoned musicians - sits poised with instruments in hand, eyes fixed on the sheet music. Despite their technical skill, they're unfamiliar with this specific piece and the conductor's vision for it.

At this stage, the maestro assumes full command, offering step-by-step instructions, setting the tempo, and clarifying how each section should interpret the score. The focus is not on discussion or improvisation but on alignment and precision. The musicians, though talented, require direction to bring a unified sound to life.

Likewise, in leadership, the Directing style is best used when individuals are new to the task at hand. It provides structure and clarity, ensuring early progress while gradually building team confidence.

Coaching

After a few rehearsals, the orchestra begins to find its rhythm. The musicians are more confident with the notes, but challenges still arise; timing inconsistencies, interpretation differences, moments of hesitation.

At this stage, the maestro shifts from strict instruction to a more collaborative approach. He engages in discussions, listens to feedback, and invites suggestions on interpretation and dynamics.

The musicians don't need to be told what to do at every moment; they need support, encouragement, and refinement.

This reflects the Coaching leadership style: a blend of high direction and high support. The leader still guides the team but does so while actively involving others in the process, building confidence and buy-in through mutual respect.

Supporting

As the concert approaches, the musicians are no longer just a group of skilled individuals; they have become a cohesive, synchronized ensemble. The music flows with shared purpose and mutual trust.

Now, the maestro steps back, allowing the musicians more freedom and ownership of their roles. He offers encouragement and subtle suggestions but avoids over-directing. The leadership focus shifts to empowerment, while trusting the team's abilities and staying present to fine-tune the final product.

This is the essence of the Supporting style. The leader becomes a sounding board, offering emotional support and occasional guidance as the team moves toward independent excellence.

Delegating

It's the night of the concert. The musicians play with unwavering confidence, filling the hall with resonance and precision. Each note rises in perfect harmony—not from control, but from trust.

The maestro barely lifts a hand. With only subtle gestures, he guides the flow, trusting the orchestra to carry the music to its full expression. The transformation is complete: the ensemble no longer needs detailed instruction; they perform as one, aligned in vision and purpose.

In this Delegating phase, the leader steps back, providing minimal direction while offering quiet confidence in the team's capability. It's not absence, it's presence without interference. Leadership becomes a gentle force behind empowered excellence.

The Power of Adaptability in Leadership

A leader's true strength lies in knowing when to step forward and when to step back. Whether guiding a new team, nurturing developing talent, or empowering seasoned performers, leaders must shift fluidly between Directing, Coaching, Supporting, and Delegating.

No team stays in one stage forever; people evolve, circumstances shift, and new challenges emerge. Situational leadership provides a dynamic framework, allowing leaders to meet their teams where they are, with exactly the right balance of clarity and autonomy. When adaptability becomes second nature, leadership transforms from mere management into art: precise, responsive, and deeply human.

Becoming the Conductor of Your Life Symphony

Every great orchestra needs a conductor. Without one, the music becomes scattered. In your life, you are that conductor. Your role is to bring together the different sections of your personal orchestra: your Strengths, Weaknesses, Opportunities, and Threats, and lead them in harmony.

Self-leadership means not only recognizing these instruments within you but also knowing how to manage, balance, and blend them. When you step into the role of conductor, you transform scattered sounds into a personal symphony that inspires and uplifts.

Tuning Your Strengths

Your strengths are the instruments that define your signature sound. They are your talents, values, passions, knowledge, and skills; the areas where you naturally shine.

But even the finest violin will sound poor if left untuned. Your strengths must be nurtured, sharpened, and aligned with purpose. Neglect dulls them; practice refines them.

- Identify your top five strengths.
- Invest in developing them through practice, feedback, and learning.
- Position them where they serve best; let your creativity lead in problem-solving, let your discipline anchor your habits, let your empathy guide your relationships.

When tuned and played with integrity, your strengths will carry the melody of your life.

Managing Weaknesses

Weaknesses are not failures. They are simply instruments that require more attention. The mistake is not having them - it's ignoring them.

- Acknowledge them with honesty. *Pretending they don't exist only creates discord.*
- Decide whether to improve them (through practice and growth) or manage them (by surrounding yourself with others whose strengths complement yours).
- Allow them to play a supportive role, not the lead.

Seizing Opportunities

Opportunities bring novelty, challenge, and excitement to the performance.

- Scan your environment regularly for new opportunities that lead you to your goals.
- Align opportunities with your core strengths and purpose.
- Embrace opportunities when they come, but ensure they integrate with the greater piece of your life.

Opportunities, when seized at the right time, transform your life's melody into a masterpiece.

Addressing Threats

You cannot control all threats, but you can prepare for them. A skilled conductor anticipates challenges and leads the orchestra with calm resilience, ensuring the music continues.

- Identify the external risks: financial pressures, toxic environments, distractions, or habits.
- Develop contingency plans.
- Stay alert; threats should be managed, not magnified.

Acknowledging threats reduces their power; preparing for them silences their disruption.

Conducting the Symphony

Strengths, weaknesses, opportunities, and threats are not separate lists; they are sections of the same orchestra. Your task as a maestro is to bring them into balance:

- Let strengths lead the melody.
- Keep weaknesses in check, offering support where needed.
- Introduce opportunities at the right time.
- Guard against threats to protect the harmony.
- When integrated, your life produces music instead of noise.

Your personal symphony is not defined by one instrument alone, but by the harmony of all.

Step onto the podium of your life. Lead with courage.
It's time to orchestrate your personal symphony.

Chapter 4

How Your Thoughts Can Impact Your Growth

As we move through life's different stages and experiences, we are continuously exposed to a range of beliefs, influences, and ideas. These exposures shape how we see ourselves and the world, ultimately influencing how we act, react, and move forward. They play a pivotal role in determining the direction and quality of our growth.

On your journey of self-development and mastery, it's important to recognize that while certain thoughts or ideas can be motivating and transformative, they can also become limiting, especially when misunderstood or taken to extremes. True growth calls for both an open mind and a balanced perspective.

Our thoughts are not random. They are shaped by how we process our experiences, emotions, memories, and surroundings. This internal lens - our paradigm - guides how we interpret events and impacts every decision we make, every step we take.

Every thought is a seed. It can either grow into a tree of opportunity or solidify into a wall that blocks your progress. When you begin to shift how you think, you also begin to see differently, and in that moment, new paths emerge.

Often, a paradigm shift begins with a spark: a realization that shakes your current belief system and invites you to consider something new. This experience can be thrilling, eye-opening, and deeply liberating, but it can also feel uncomfortable. Growth sometimes demands that we step beyond our comfort zones, confront uncertainty, and release long-held mental patterns that no longer serve us.

While embracing new ways of thinking can be powerful and transformative, it's just as important to avoid extremes. Overanalyzing every thought or becoming overly attached to a single perspective can create stress or blind spots. True growth lies in adaptability; in learning to stay open to change while remaining rooted in clarity and intention.

Growth is not a straight path but a continuous cycle: learning, unlearning, and relearning. Your thoughts shape your perception, but it's your ability to pair insight with action, openness with discernment, and courage with flexibility that leads to meaningful transformation.

Thoughts & Life

Before we can master our thoughts, we must first understand their relationship to life itself. Life is not simply the passing of time; it's a dynamic canvas filled with experiences, lessons, and evolving opportunities. It calls us not just to exist, but to engage.

Thinking about life is more than reflection; it's an act of self-exploration. It helps us define what matters, notice the beauty in everyday moments, and align our choices with a deeper sense of purpose. Through this awareness, we learn to embrace change, honour the present, and pursue growth with intention.

Life is unpredictable and precious; a journey marked by highs, lows, stillness, and momentum. Yet one truth always holds: while we cannot control every outcome, we can choose how we show up, respond, and evolve through it all.

As we move through our individual journeys, we often pause to ask life's deeper questions:

- What is the purpose of our existence?
- What truly brings us joy and fulfilment?
- What values and beliefs define who we are?

These aren't questions with one-size-fits-all answers. They're deeply personal and evolving, shaped by our experiences, moments of reflection, and willingness to grow. The way we choose to live each day ultimately defines the richness and meaning of our lives.

Thoughts & What Matters Most

Life moves fast; a constant stream of decisions, responsibilities, and shifting priorities. In the midst of chasing goals or trying to meet expectations, it's easy to lose sight of what genuinely matters.

But when we pause, step back, and reflect, we often find that true fulfillment isn't found in titles, possessions, or achievements. It lives in the quality of our connections, the principles we live by, and the quiet moments when our actions align with our inner truth.

What matters most isn't always loud or visible; it's often subtle, steady, and deeply rooted in the heart.

What Matters Most

At the core of a meaningful life are the people, principles, and priorities that shape who we are. While what we value most will differ from person to person, certain foundational elements tend to resonate across all lives:

- **Relationships**: The deep connections we share with family, friends, and loved ones offer belonging, support, and emotional grounding.
- **Purpose & Passion**: The pursuits that spark our enthusiasm and remind us why we get up each day - the work or causes that feel meaningful.
- **Health & Well-being**: Without tending to our physical, mental, and emotional health, even our greatest accomplishments can feel empty.
- **Time & Presence**: Choosing to be present rather than always rushing to the next thing.

These pillars form the roots of fulfillment. When we neglect them, even the most celebrated successes can leave us feeling disconnected or restless. True happiness begins when we realign with what matters most.

Living in Alignment with What Matters

When we pause to reflect on what truly matters, we begin to realign our actions with our deepest values. This reflection creates a path toward living more deliberately, where each choice serves a greater sense of meaning.

- **Clarifying Our Values**: What core principles shape our decisions? Are we living in alignment with them or just reacting to demands?
- **Savouring the Simple Joys**: Fulfillment often hides in the quiet moments; a shared laugh, a peaceful morning, or a deep conversation.
- **Choosing Intentionally**: Are we investing time in what feeds our spirit, or being swept up by distractions that offer only momentary relief?

Being present and living with intention doesn't happen by default - it's a choice. The more we protect what matters, the more space we create for joy, peace, and connection. When we ignore these essentials, we often feel a lingering emptiness that success alone can't cure.

When we recognize what's important before urgency dictates our choices, we empower ourselves to prioritize with clarity and purpose. It's the difference between reacting and choosing, between surviving and living with purpose. Ultimately, a meaningful life is not defined by what we accumulate, but by what we contribute. It's not measured by how busy we are, but by how present we are, and not by how much we accomplish, but by how deeply we connect.

I Think ... Therefore, I Am.

It is through thinking that we make sense of the world around us—our relationships, our experiences, our successes, and even our struggles. Thoughts are the notes created by the thinking process. And like notes, they come together to form melodies that shape our paradigms. Those paradigms, in turn, influence how we act, react, and ultimately interact with the consequences of our choices.

Throughout my own journey, I have travelled across six continents, met people from different walks of life, and experienced cultures as diverse as the instruments of an orchestra. In every role I have played - whether as a son, a brother, a husband, a father, a friend, a leader, a team member, a coach, a teacher, or a consultant - I have carried with me thoughts. Some were shaped by personal experiences; the wisdom of those around me sparked others. They were not always tied to specific events, but often emerged as reflections, questions, or insights - seeds of guidance that helped me think deeper.

Thoughts are open to interpretation, discussion, and even debate. They are not absolute truths; they are starting points for reflection. You don't have to agree with every thought, but you can analyze them, relate them to your own life, and perhaps discover new meanings. After all, some of the most profound compositions in history were inspired by themes borrowed, reimagined, or passed down by others.

As the philosopher René Descartes famously said: "I think, therefore I am." Thinking affirms our existence, but it also invites us to share our inner music with others. By expressing your thoughts, you may offer someone a perspective that changes the course of their life.

The Power of Thinking

Thinking allows us to expand our awareness. By analyzing, questioning, and reflecting, we deepen our understanding and broaden our perspective. When challenges arise, it is our ability to think critically and creatively that helps us compose solutions. Thinking allows us to weigh options, consider alternatives, and choose actions that align with our goals and values. In this way, thinking becomes the rhythm that guides our decisions.

Reflective thinking helps us tune our inner instruments. It allows us to process emotions, recognize patterns, and challenge unhelpful thoughts. This self-awareness builds resilience, balance, and positive mental health.

Thoughts Are The Seed of Action

At its core, every action begins with a thought. Thoughts are the seeds from which our behaviours grow. Just as no symphony begins without notes on a page, no achievement or transformation begins without the spark of thought. When nurtured and directed, these seeds grow into melodies that not only shape our own lives but also resonate in the lives of others.

So, think deeply. Think critically. Think creatively. And above all, share your thoughts, because the music you create in your mind today may become the inspiration that transforms someone else's tomorrow.

"Freedom is a FREE offer!"

"Freedom is free; when we accept it, we also accept the responsibilities that come with it."

Freedom is not absolute. It exists within boundaries and is governed by principles that ensure its sustainability. To enjoy freedom fully, we must understand that it operates under structure, not chaos.

Think of it like playing a sport. When we choose to play any ball game, we accept the rules of that game, the limits of the field, the roles of the players, and the consequences of fouls. If we don't like those rules, we can choose another game. What we can't do is demand a soccer match be played with a basketball hoop or allow players to use their hands instead of their feet. That wouldn't be soccer anymore.

Of course, rules can evolve. But any proposed changes must align with the essence of the game. In the same way, freedom can grow and adapt, but only when we respect its foundational truths. Otherwise, what we call "freedom" becomes disorder.

With freedom comes responsibility, not just to ourselves, but to the people and world around us. Every decision we make carries weight, and true freedom demands that we stay mindful of how our actions affect others.

Freedom is not a license to harm, disrespect, or disregard the rights of others. It cannot stand alone as a selfish entitlement. Instead, it must be understood as part of an interconnected system, where your liberty and mine coexist in delicate balance.

> *The only freedom that is truly limitless is the freedom to choose. What follows those choices, however, is never free of consequence.*

Without structure, freedom becomes chaos. That's why every system that honors freedom must also uphold accountability. When we act, we must be prepared to accept the outcomes of our decisions and ensure they're consequences we're willing to live with.

"We are independent only within the limitations of the dynamics of our interdependent environment."

We often take pride in our independence; our ability to make choices, pursue goals, and shape our own paths. Yet, much like freedom, independence doesn't exist in isolation. It is influenced - and at times constrained - by the web of relationships and systems that surround us. Whether through family, work, culture, or society, our autonomy is in constant negotiation with the world around us.

The Role of Interdependence
Family: The Foundation of Support

In a family, each member plays a vital role in sustaining emotional, psychological, and practical balance. While we may feel autonomous in our decisions, it's often the love, guidance, and safety provided by our family that makes those choices possible. Independence isn't forged in isolation, it is often nurtured within the invisible arms of support that hold us up.

The Workplace: Collaboration

No one works in complete isolation. Each role contributes to a shared objective, and the performance of one individual inevitably impacts the success of others. Even when you have the autonomy to carry out tasks independently, your work is part of a collective whole. Independence within a team isn't about working alone, it's about understanding how your efforts align with, and support the larger structure around you.

Recognizing that we are independent only within the framework of interdependence invites us to see the full picture. It's not about losing our individuality, but about becoming aware of the systems that shape our choices and amplify our efforts. True independence is not about detachment, but about navigating the delicate balance between personal autonomy and purposeful connection.

"We're all different in how we see and do things, yet we share meaningful points of connection."

"The way we bring our differences together is key to creating harmony."

We each perceive, think, and act in unique ways. Yet, beneath our differences, there are shared values, ideas, and hopes that unite us.

Picture a puzzle: each piece has its own shape, color, and edge, but none can complete the picture alone. Every piece contributes to the whole. If just one is missing, the image is incomplete. The beauty of the puzzle comes not from sameness, but from how the differences come together to form something greater.

Now, imagine an orchestra. Every musician plays a different instrument, each producing its own sound and rhythm. If they played alone or without coordination, the result would be noise. If they all played the same note, it would lack richness. But when their distinct sounds are orchestrated together, they create music far more powerful than any single part.

The goal is not to erase our differences but to align them in ways that build something stronger. Individual talent is valuable, but collaboration multiplies that value. True success emerges when our differences complement one another and lead to shared impact.

The art of harmony lies not in uniformity, but in unity with purpose.

"Everything is relative and subject to people's Paradigm."

Our understanding of the world is not based on objective facts alone, but on how we interpret those facts. These interpretations stem from our paradigms, shaped by our upbringing, culture, education, emotions, past experiences, and even our current mood.

Unless two people share the same position, background, and context, they are bound to see things differently. But different doesn't mean wrong, it means each perspective is filtered through a different life story.

What one person sees as right, another may question. What feels just to one may seem unfair to someone else. Our judgments, choices, and assumptions are grounded in individual frameworks that are as distinct as our fingerprints.

No single perspective can claim full ownership of the truth. Growth begins when we accept that multiple truths can exist at once. Rather than dismissing what we don't understand, we become wiser by choosing curiosity, empathy, and the willingness to see through someone else's lens.

Allowing ourselves to shift our paradigm is essential for broadening our perspective. It opens the door to deeper empathy, better decision-making, and more meaningful relationships.

At its heart, embracing the relativity of perspectives doesn't mean abandoning our core beliefs; it means expanding them. It's the understanding that truth can be multifaceted, and that every new viewpoint we engage with adds depth and dimension to our own.

By recognizing the value in other perspectives, we cultivate a more flexible, compassionate, and wise way of seeing the world and of showing up in it.

"Challenges become obstacles if you see them in isolation of the opportunities that lie ahead."

When we encounter difficulty, it often feels overwhelming, frustrating, disorienting, or even paralyzing. But the real limitation arises not from the challenge itself, but from our perception of it. If we fixate solely on the problem, we risk narrowing our vision, missing the possibilities that adversity can bring to light.

Challenges, when viewed in isolation, become walls. But when we widen our perspective, those same challenges can serve as doorways, leading to new growth, deeper resilience, and unforeseen innovations.

Take the COVID-19 pandemic. In-person learning, once a staple of education, was abruptly disrupted. This could have stalled progress entirely. Instead, educators and students around the world pivoted, turning to digital platforms that expanded access, introduced flexible learning models, and redefined the boundaries of the classroom.

Think about a time in your own life when a door seemed to slam shut. At first, the rejection feels frustrating and disheartening. But when you pause and widen your perspective, you may notice that the setback pushed you to refine your skills, expand your network, or pursue an opportunity you wouldn't have considered otherwise. What first felt like a challenge became the doorway to growth and alignment with something better.

"The Illusion of Perfection"

"Perfection is not a destination—it's a distraction."

No one is flawless, and the pursuit of flawlessness often leads not to fulfilment but to frustration, self-doubt, and burnout. Rather than spending our energy trying to smooth out every imperfection, we can begin to see them as essential to our individuality. Just as a handwoven rug bears subtle variations that make it unique, or a melody carries offbeat notes that make it unforgettable, our imperfections give us character, depth, and authenticity.

When we accept people as they are - not as idealized versions we've imagined - they feel seen. They feel safe. And in that space of acceptance, true connection is born. Everyone carries a mix of strengths, flaws, and aspirations. When we release the pressure to be perfect, we make room for people to grow, explore, and contribute freely.

This mindset shift isn't just personal, it's transformational in how we lead and influence others. Great leaders, teachers, and mentors don't aim to shape flawless people. They guide others to discover and express their strengths, even in the presence of imperfection. Their gift is not perfectionism, but perspective.

A great musician doesn't strive to hit every note with mechanical precision. What moves us is the emotion behind the sound, the tremble of vulnerability, the surge of passion, the sincerity in each imperfect phrase. That is what makes it unforgettable. And so it is with us.

A wise leader doesn't demand flawlessness from their team. Instead, they recognize each person's strengths and help navigate weaknesses, building toward shared success through collaboration, not control.

Similarly, a lasting relationship isn't held together by perfection, but by mutual acceptance, patience, and understanding. When we try to "fix" others, we may cross the line into control. But when we embrace their imperfections alongside our own, we foster trust, resilience, and authenticity.

The power we hold - whether as leaders, partners, friends, or mentors - does not come from sculpting perfection. It comes from standing in the truth of imperfection, choosing compassion over criticism, and making room for growth without judgment.

In accepting and working with imperfection, we don't lower the bar, we deepen the connection. We cultivate empathy. And we create space for meaningful progress, both in ourselves and in others.

"Feeling fulfilled is about appreciating what you already have, rather than endlessly chasing what's missing."

We live in a world that constantly urges us to strive for more; to do more, have more, and become more. It's easy to believe that fulfillment is always just one achievement away. We tell ourselves that the next milestone, promotion, or possession will finally make us feel complete.

But true fulfillment doesn't live in the future. It begins in the present. It's rooted in your ability to pause, reflect, and value what's already within reach.

While dreams and ambitions matter, they're only part of the picture. If we only focus on what's missing, we widen the gap between where we are and where we think happiness lives. But when we shift our perspective and recognize the meaning in our current moments - growth, connection, effort - we open the door to lasting contentment.

A fulfilled life isn't about standing still. It's about walking the path with joy, not just rushing toward the destination.

We don't exist in isolation. Our deepest sense of meaning often comes from how we relate to others through family, friendships, community, and the impact we make. Fulfillment is born from recognizing our place in something larger than ourselves.

Fulfilment is not a destination you arrive at. It's a way of thinking. A way of living. It emerges when you embrace gratitude, stay present in the process, and understand the significance of your unique role in the world. That's the kind of fulfilment no trophy or title can give, and no failure can take away.

"We cannot change people!"
"We can only choose to provide them with the knowledge and environment that facilitates their decision to change."

Sustainable transformation can't be forced; it must arise from personal will. Imagine a garden: you can't rush a flower into blooming by tugging at its petals. But by providing sunlight, water, and care, you create conditions where growth is possible.

People evolve when they find meaningful reasons to do so, when the hope of change outweighs the ease of staying the same. By sharing insight, modelling growth, and cultivating a supportive space, we plant seeds of possibility. But only the individual can choose to make them grow.

Forcing change leads only to temporary compliance, not lasting growth. When someone shifts their behaviour out of pressure or obligation, that change rarely endures; it often disappears as soon as the external force is removed. True transformation happens when a person sees the value for themselves and takes ownership of the journey.

Often, people resist change because their worldview has been shaped by different values, experiences, or emotional histories. Their priorities might not match what we envision for them, and that doesn't make them wrong. Growth isn't about conformity; it's about honoring the freedom to evolve in one's own time and way.

While change is ultimately a personal responsibility, we can still serve a vital role. By being a steady presence, offering knowledge, and creating a space of encouragement, we light the path, but the decision to walk it must be theirs.

"You can't force things in common; otherwise, you risk creating a short-lived, artificial connection."

"What we can genuinely share is a commitment to respecting, celebrating, and supporting our differences."

Many people assume that meaningful relationships rely on shared interests: listening to the same music, enjoying the same shows, or participating in the same hobbies. While these moments can create surface-level bonding, a real connection isn't rooted in sameness. It's born from mutual respect, genuine appreciation, and the willingness to embrace one another's uniqueness.

It's easy to confuse "having something in common" with "doing things together." But authentic connection comes from shared meaning, not necessarily shared preferences. What draws people closer is not always what they do together, but why they do it and how they show up for one another.

Sometimes we engage in activities that we don't particularly enjoy - watching a show for a loved one, attending an event for a friend - not because we love the experience itself, but because we cherish the joy it brings to them. In the end, it's not the act but the intention behind it that forges a deeper connection. That intention is what makes relationships meaningful and lasting.

Trying to mold a relationship around sameness often leads to a temporary connection that eventually feels forced and draining.

When we chase after common interests simply to feel more aligned, we may find fleeting comfort, but not lasting depth.

Imagine an orchestra: Each instrument has its own voice, rhythm, and purpose. A violin doesn't pretend to be a trumpet, and the drum doesn't imitate the piano. Yet together, they produce a symphony; a unified, beautiful sound that depends on their differences, not their sameness. In relationships, the goal isn't to become identical, but to find harmony in contrast.

Celebrating our differences isn't just an ideal; it's a necessity for sustainable connection. True belonging isn't about fitting into someone else's mold; it's about being seen, valued, and loved as we are. When we honor one another's uniqueness, we create the kind of relationship that doesn't just survive - but harmonizes.

"You Are Defined by Your Own Actions"

We often say, "Actions speak louder than words" - and they do. No matter how much we claim to love, support, or believe in something, those words lose power if our actions contradict them.

Our choices - how we show up, keep our promises, or respond to others - reveal far more about us than our declarations ever could. They reflect our character, values, and priorities. Even small actions carry weight, especially when repeated over time.

People place their trust not in what we say, but in what we do consistently. Love isn't just a feeling; it's a verb. It's found in kindness, patience, and presence. Saying "I love you" means little when our behaviour tells a different story. Likewise, calling ourselves trustworthy rings hollow when we don't follow through.

Who we are is defined not by our intentions alone, but by the lived expression of those intentions.

We all have the power to shape our identity through our actions. Every time we choose honesty over deception, or compassion over cruelty, we contribute to the larger story of who we are becoming.

Unlike words, which can be forgotten or misinterpreted, our actions leave an impression that often lasts far longer. They shape how others see us, and how we see ourselves. When we act with intention, aligning behaviour with values, we not only build self-trust but also inspire trust in others.

By being mindful of how our choices ripple outward, we create a legacy built not on performance, but on genuine character. And while words may set the tone, it is our actions that define the music of our lives.

"Only when we separate ourselves from our pride & ego, we would be able to see our true self."

Pride and ego act like tinted lenses, distorting how we view ourselves and the world around us. They may inflate our self-image or blind us to our weaknesses, making honest self-reflection difficult. Until we learn to step outside these filters, we risk mistaking illusion for truth.

Pride often keeps us from admitting mistakes, feeding our desire for validation and masking our vulnerabilities. Ego, meanwhile, can create a false sense of superiority that isolates us from others and undermines empathy.

While a healthy sense of self is important, unchecked ego leads to arrogance, disconnection, and conflict. Self-confidence is grounded in genuine ability and self-respect; ego, by contrast, often grows out of insecurity and a need to defend our image. Learning the difference allows us to cultivate humility without losing strength.

True self-awareness is rooted in humility. This doesn't mean downplaying our accomplishments or ignoring our worth; it means being honest about both our strengths and our limitations.

We don't exist in isolation, we're part of an interconnected world. Understanding this helps us see the ways we impact others and are, in turn, shaped by them. When we release the defences that pride and ego build, we open ourselves to deeper connection, mutual learning, and more authentic relationships.

To truly see ourselves, we must be willing to shed the illusions that ego creates. This journey asks for courage; courage to own our strengths, face our flaws, and live as our whole, unguarded selves.

"Don't judge the elephant for its inability to climb the tree!"

Imagine holding an elephant to the standard of a monkey, expecting it to climb with agility, then labelling it a failure when it cannot. It sounds absurd, yet we do this with people all the time. We judge others through the narrow lens of abilities we deem important, often ignoring the very strengths that make them exceptional.

Each of us is built differently with distinct skills, instincts, and limitations. When we measure someone by a standard misaligned with their design, we not only dismiss their potential but also reinforce limiting, unfair narratives.

Instead of focusing on what someone lacks, what if we asked: *What is their element? Where do they shine?* True fairness lies in acknowledging individual strengths, not in forcing everyone to climb the same tree.

Consider how easily we overlook the brilliance of those around us simply because we're focused on the wrong metrics:

- A student who struggles with math but creates breathtaking art.
- An employee who designs captivating presentations but dreads speaking in front of a crowd.
- A person who expresses deep love through quiet gestures rather than spoken words.

If we judge these individuals solely by their shortcomings, we miss the full picture of who they are and what they bring to the table.

Rather than forcing people into predefined molds, we should build spaces that recognize and nurture their natural strengths. True success happens when people are allowed to thrive in their element, not when they're pressured to conform to someone else's script.

So, shift your gaze. Instead of asking, *"Why can't they climb the tree?"* ask, *"Where do they run free?"* That's where their power lives.

"Be careful what you wish for!"

"What sparkles on the outside may hide splinters beneath the shine."

We're often drawn to things that appear beautiful on the surface: a dream job, a perfect relationship, a glamorous lifestyle. But not everything that glitters is gold. Like a rose with hidden thorns, beauty can mask deeper truths, and desire can blind us to what lies beneath.

- **The Illusion of the Perfect Partner**: A charming, attractive partner may seem like the answer to your dreams. But if the relationship lacks trust, compassion, or mutual respect, that charm eventually crumbles, revealing a foundation built on illusion.

- **The Dream Job That Became a Cage**: Prestige and a big paycheck might be seductive. But if the cost is your peace of mind, your health, or your values, the dream can quickly turn into something hollow - beautiful from afar but bruising up close.

Be mindful. Not every wish is worth chasing, especially when the price is damaging.

Ask yourself before chasing what dazzles:

- What will this truly cost me?
- Am I seeing the full picture, or only the parts that shine?

- Does this desire align with my values, or am I being seduced by surface appeal?

True wisdom is found not in chasing beauty, but in seeing beyond it. Just like a castle built on weak foundations, anything lacking depth and integrity will eventually collapse, no matter how grand it seems.

> *Be careful what you wish for, because getting it means inheriting every consequence that comes with it, seen and unseen.*

Chapter 5

The Fine Line

Language is powerful. But it's not just about the words we use; it's about the meaning, intention, and delivery behind them. There is a fine line in communication: a subtle but critical balance between what is said and what is meant. This distinction matters because words can be interpreted in vastly different ways depending on tone, context, and delivery.

We see this fine line crossed very often on television debates, in group discussions, or casual conversations. An opinion shared with care and a genuine intent to invite dialogue can open the door to meaningful exchange. But the same thought, delivered harshly or without regard for others' perspectives, can come across as dismissive, offensive, or even hostile.

Framing your thoughts constructively rather than confrontationally is key. It ensures your message is received rather than rejected. A comment meant to build a connection or express concern can be easily misinterpreted when phrased bluntly or delivered without sensitivity to the recipient's emotional landscape.

When Words Cross the Line

Words have weight, and their impact depends heavily on how they are spoken. Misunderstandings often arise when:

- We are too blunt, prioritizing directness over tact.
- We offer unsolicited advice.
- We speak at the wrong time, ignoring the emotional state of the listener.
- We use words that may be perceived as dismissive or condescending.

Mastering the fine line means becoming more intentional with our words. It's not about suppressing honesty, but about delivering truth in a way that invites understanding rather than defensiveness. When we speak with awareness and care, we open space for healthier dialogue, where words don't just convey meaning, but also nurture relationships.

Freedom and Chaos: When Liberty Loses Structure

Freedom is one of society's most cherished values, but it is not limitless. True freedom exists within a framework of rules and responsibilities that uphold fairness, safety, and harmony. Without structure, freedom can quickly spiral into chaos, where personal liberties are used without regard for others, resulting in instability and division. The challenge lies in understanding where freedom ends and chaos begins.

A Balance of Rights and Responsibilities

Freedom isn't simply the space to express oneself, it also includes the duty to respect the rights of others and the laws that sustain social order. When honoured, freedom nurtures diversity, creativity, and progress. But the absence of boundaries doesn't expand freedom; it diminishes it by opening the door to unpredictability and harm.

Chaos arises when freedom is exercised without regard for its consequences. Factors contributing to this shift include:

- The absence of laws and regulations
- Disregard for shared social norms
- Lack of personal accountability
- Rising social and economic inequality

Just as sports require rules to ensure fair play, a society needs structure to prevent harm while allowing individuality to thrive. Boundaries do not weaken freedom - they preserve it.

True freedom is the ability to make personal choices while honouring the limits that protect others.

Freedom & Independence: What's the Difference?

Freedom and independence are often used interchangeably, but they're not the same. Freedom is the ability to act, speak, or think without unnecessary restriction. Independence, on the other hand, is the capacity to support oneself without external aid or control. Understanding how these concepts differ helps us better grasp what it truly means to live autonomously.

Freedom Within Dependence

It's a common assumption that freedom and independence must coexist; that one cannot be free unless entirely self-reliant. But in reality, freedom can exist within structures of dependence.

A child may be free to choose their clothes, hobbies, or academic interests, even while remaining financially and emotionally dependent on their parents. Likewise, employees might enjoy decision-making freedom within their roles, while still relying on employers for income, direction, and job security.

These examples show that freedom is often contextually shaped, not just by autonomy, but by the environment in which it's exercised. Independence may strengthen freedom, but it is not always required for it to exist.

Many young people often say they want to be "free," when what they truly seek is independence - the power to make decisions without external interference. Independence can expand one's freedom by reducing dependence on others, but it does not guarantee absolute freedom.

Freedom and Independence Are Never Absolute

Neither freedom nor independence exists in a vacuum. Both operate within the frameworks of the systems we belong to: our families, schools, workplaces, communities, and governments.

The goal isn't to escape all structure, but to be intentional about the environments we engage with. True autonomy lies in choosing systems that align with our values and navigating them with awareness. When we understand the limitations we accept, and the reasons behind them, we can exercise freedom and independence in ways that are grounded, sustainable, and personally meaningful.

Criticism & Insult

Criticism is not insult - they come from fundamentally different places. Criticism is intended to express concern, offer feedback, or suggest improvements. It's focused on growth. An insult, on the other hand, is meant to belittle, attack, or emotionally wound.

The fine line between the two often lies in the speaker's intent, the emotional tone behind the words, and how the message is delivered. Criticism can easily slip into insult when it becomes vague, disrespectful, emotionally charged, or personal. While constructive criticism invites change, an insult shuts down communication and damages trust.

How Criticism Becomes an Insult

Criticism focuses on behavior or output; insults attack the person. Saying, *"Your report had a few errors, but here's how you can improve it,"* gives direction and keeps the conversation professional. Saying, *"You're terrible at writing reports,"* offers no guidance and targets the person, not the problem.

Constructive criticism is specific; insults are often vague and exaggerated. *"Your presentation could be more engaging if you used visual aids."* provides a clear path for improvement. In contrast, *"That was the worst presentation I've ever seen"* is dismissive and offers nothing useful.

Consider a conversation between two colleagues discussing remote work. One says, *"I believe working remotely is more productive because it saves commuting time."* A respectful response might sound like: *"I see your point, but I think remote work weakens collaboration. I'd suggest more in-person meetings to balance things out."* This is criticism; it engages with the idea, offers perspective, and even suggests a constructive path forward. But if the reply shifts to, *"You're an idiot if you think remote work is productive,"* the line is crossed. The focus moves from the idea being debated to an attack on the person expressing it, shutting down dialogue and eroding trust.

Criticism is respectful; insults are condescending. Tone and word choice matter. Effective feedback can be direct and firm, but it should never be laced with sarcasm, mockery, or humiliation. Respect invites change, while disrespect shuts it down.

Criticism is solution-oriented. Insults aim to hurt. When the goal is to help, feedback should highlight the issue and suggest a path forward. Pointing out flaws without offering direction does little more than discourage.

Avoid reacting defensively, even if the feedback feels personal.

By staying respectful, aiming for solutions, and managing emotional reactions, we can make sure our feedback helps rather than harms.

Self-Confidence vs. Arrogance

Self-confidence and arrogance can appear similar on the surface; both may involve assertiveness, bold opinions, and a belief in one's abilities. But their foundations, impact, and mindset couldn't be more different. Recognizing the difference is vital for nurturing healthy self-esteem without damaging relationships.

What Sets Them Apart?

Self-confidence is rooted in a grounded understanding of one's strengths and limitations. Confident individuals trust themselves but remain teachable. They admit mistakes, welcome feedback, and uplift others without feeling threatened.

Arrogance, in contrast, arises from an inflated sense of superiority. Arrogant individuals often overstate their capabilities and ignore their flaws. They may belittle others, reject guidance, and expect special treatment. Unchecked arrogance can lead to isolation, resentment, and missed opportunities.

True confidence isn't about proving superiority, it's about trusting in your worth without diminishing the worth of others. When we believe in ourselves while honoring those around us, we build stronger connections, inspire growth, and move forward with purpose.

Final Notes

Orchestrating Your Growth

As we draw this journey to a close, envision yourself not just as a participant in life, but as its conductor. With every movement, you shape these elements into a symphony that is wholly your own. The baton is in your hand. The stage is set. The world awaits the story only you can tell.

Through these chapters, you've gathered the tools to embrace self-awareness, thrive in collaboration, and lead with authenticity. But the true magic lies in how you transform these lessons through the lens of your own voice and vision. Let your music echo with your deepest values, with the courage of your trials and the triumph of your growth.

Play boldly. Lead with purpose. And compose a harmony that not only elevates your present but becomes a lasting melody echoing through lives and generations far beyond your own.

Pause & Reflect

In the journey of growth, pausing isn't a detour, it's part of the path. Moving forward matters but so does knowing *why* and *where* you're going. Without reflection, progress can become directionless.

Reflection helps us assess how far we've come, recalibrate our goals, and make purposeful adjustments. In academics, a student may discover that a different major aligns more closely with their passions, or that adding a second major or self-learning new skills unlocks a more authentic path.

In the professional world, reflection might reveal a need for upskilling, a shift in industry, or adapting to emerging technologies to remain relevant and fulfilled.

In relationships, taking time to reflect deepens our understanding of how we show up for others. It allows us to nurture trust, resolve conflict, and strengthen bonds through conscious effort.

When we fail to pause, we risk burnout, repetition, and disconnection from our purpose. Growth isn't a matter of speed or accumulation, it's about learning with intention and choosing a path that resonates with who we're becoming.

The Art of Orchestrating Growth

Growth doesn't happen by accident, it's an intentional process grounded in planning, self-awareness, and adaptability. Each stage of your personal, educational, and professional evolution has its own rhythm. Recognizing and managing these stages ensures that you're not just advancing, but building something lasting.

Tuning Your Instruments – Self-Discovery

At the outset of any meaningful journey, clarity is essential. This is the moment to tune inward. Discover your strengths, identify your weaknesses, and uncover what truly matters to you: your values, passions, and core beliefs. Without this internal tuning, any external progress risks sounding off-key.

Playing in Harmony – Collaboration & Growth

Once you've established clarity, it's time to step into shared spaces. Like instruments aligning in harmony, collaboration demands communication, trust, and mutual purpose. This stage is where you refine your ability to contribute to collective success while continuing your individual development.

Lead With Impact

As you grow, you begin to take on leadership roles; stepping into the role of the conductor. At this stage, you guide others, coordinate efforts, and make decisions that influence not just your journey but the journeys of those around you. Effective leadership requires more than authority; it calls for vision, empathy, and the ability to bring out the best in others.

Being the conductor means understanding each member of the ensemble; leveraging their unique strengths, aligning them with shared goals, and harmonizing effort toward a larger purpose.

Avoiding Pitfalls in Your Growth Journey

As you orchestrate your path forward, it's important to watch for common missteps that can derail progress:

- **Skipping Stages**: Attempting to lead without developing self-awareness or gaining collaborative experience often results in disconnection and ineffective leadership. Each stage lays the foundation for the next.

- **Resisting Change**: Growth isn't always comfortable. It often asks you to step outside familiar territory, embrace uncertainty, and acquire new skills. Avoiding change can limit your potential.
- **Failing to Reflect**: Without intentional reflection, you risk repeating the same mistakes or overlooking crucial lessons.

> *Growth depends on your ability to pause, evaluate, and adjust course.*

Orchestrating your growth means understanding that every stage of development has its own purpose and timing. Like an orchestra that produces a masterpiece through deliberate and coordinated effort, your growth becomes a living symphony composed of your evolving skills, acquired knowledge, meaningful relationships, and lived experiences.

Books That Influenced This Work

Throughout my 30-year journey of coaching, mentoring, and leading, I've been inspired by a diverse range of authors and thinkers whose work has left a lasting impact on my understanding of personal growth, leadership, and human potential. While the ideas in this book are rooted in my lived experience, many of them were clarified, challenged, or enriched through the wisdom I encountered in the pages of the following books:

- The 7 Habits of Highly Effective People by Stephen R. Covey
    A timeless framework for personal and interpersonal effectiveness that continues to guide leaders across generations.
- Man's Search for Meaning by Viktor E. Frankl
    A profound reflection on resilience, purpose, and the human spirit, especially in the face of adversity.
- The Art of Possibility by Rosamund Stone Zander & Benjamin Zander
    A transformative guide to seeing the world through a lens of possibility, creativity, and leadership, with a musical touch that deeply resonates with the metaphor of this book.
- Start With Why by Simon Sinek
    A modern-day call to purpose-driven action—reminding us that clarity of why unlocks commitment and leadership.
- The Power of Now by Eckhart Tolle
    A gentle yet powerful reminder to live in the present and listen to the stillness within.
- Good to Great by Jim Collins
    A powerful study on what separates good companies (or leaders) from great ones— introducing the "Level 5 Leader" concept.
- Leadership and the One Minute Manager by Ken Blanchard, Patricia Zigarmi, Drea Zigarmi

Introduces the Situational Leadership II (SLII) model, explaining how to adjust leadership style based on follower readiness.

- Developing the Leader Within You 2.0 by John C. Maxwell
  Touches on the need for leaders to evolve their approach depending on the situation and people involved.
- The 8th Habit: From Effectiveness to Greatness by Stephen R. Covey
  - *A powerful continuation of the 7 Habits, introducing the vital concept of finding your voice and helping others find theirs—a theme at the core of personal and collective leadership.*
- The Situational Leader by Dr. Paul Hersey
  A foundational work that presents the original Situational Leadership® model, emphasizing flexibility, clarity, and the art of matching leadership style to team readiness—a true conductor's guide to adaptive leadership.

These books, among others, helped shape my perspective. I honour them here as part of the larger symphony of voices that have echoed through my life's work.

Your Notes

www.ingramcontent.com/pod-product-compliance
Lightning Source LLC
Chambersburg PA
CBHW020415080526
44584CB00014B/1347